Common Wealth

Common Wealth

Contemporary Poets
of Virginia

Edited by
Sarah Kennedy and
R. T. Smith

University of Virginia Press
Charlottesville and London

University of Virginia Press
© 2003 by the Rector and Visitors of the University of Virginia
All rights reserved
Printed in the United States of America on acid-free paper
First published 2003

9 8 7 6 5 4 3 2 1

Library of Congress Cataloging-in-Publication Data
Common wealth : contemporary poets of Virginia / edited by Sarah Kennedy
and R. T. Smith.
    p.   cm.
  ISBN 0-8139-2222-4 (acid-free paper) — ISBN 0-8139-2223-2 (pbk. :
acid-free paper)
    1. American poetry—Virginia.   2. Virginia—Poetry.   I. Kennedy,
Sarah, Ph. D.   II. Smith, R. T.
  PS558.V5 c66 2003
  811'.60809755—dc21

2003006715

Contents

Introduction

Virginia has long been known as the birthplace of presidents and the site of the Civil War's end at Appomattox. Many know its wide-ranging topography and culture, its mountains and coastlines, its wilderness and urban sprawl. What may be less known is that the Old Dominion is home to many writers, both nationally recognized and newly emerging. Among them are a surprising number of poets, whose skill and diversity make their work crucial to any discussion of the various forms and modes that mark the poetry, or perhaps we should say "poetries," of the early twenty-first century. Why Virginia has been the birthplace of so many poets may be a mystery, but it's no secret that active engagement with poetry through readings, graduate programs, and journal publication has made the state an attractive adopted home for poets from all over the country. The books being produced by poets of Virginia are as varied as the state itself, and the writers at Hollins, Charlottesville, Blacksburg, Richmond, Northern Virginia, and Lexington—fertile poetic communities in themselves—provide stimulating creative cross-pollination for everyone who lives here. More broadly, the voices of Virginia-born poets, who now work all across the nation, can be heard within the various styles that make up contemporary poetry.

Some Virginia-born writers, not surprisingly, have remained here ' their entire careers. Claudia Emerson, born in Chatham and currently teaching at Mary Washington College, has focused her work on her home state in a way that boldly rewrites received history. Emerson's first book, *Pharaoh, Pharaoh*, recorded the details of rural Virginia life in almost mythic language. "Auction," one of the selections here, links the land with a dead woman's body: "Under her crushed narcissus, / the varicose wake of a mole heaves." This linkage, Emerson shows, is the way we see land, as the speaker, staring into a mirror, sees "the fields, / falling away from the house, steep with / distortion." "Plagues" reveals the definition that religious frames lend to the daily frustrations of farm life: "All night the orphaned / locusts wheeze in the darkness, grafted now / with disinherited language, until / we are all of one mind." And "The Admirer," a more recent poem, casts that frustration back into identification with the natural world: a woman dressing birds from an unwelcome suitor decides that "he should have left the doves / their beloved sky, for she would not be won."

Richard Dillard, too, is a native Virginian who has stayed. Born in Roanoke and now a professor at Hollins University, Dillard has not strayed far from home physically, but his work ranges into myth, as well. In "Poe at the End," Dillard weaves a portrait of an artist from the fragments of literary history, exploring the life—and death—of that mysterious quasi-Virginian who wrote "The Raven." Finally a creation of his own fiction, Poe ends up drunk and voting under "a dozen names: / His own, Usher, Reynolds, Dupin, Pym, / Raising his hand again and again, taking the oath, / Swearing he was who he was and was not, / Swearing he was." This Poe, staggering "[a]way from Virginia and toward / Virginia in the grave," has learned from the death of his cousin-wife that *"Art kills as often as it saves."* At the end of his life, however, he sees "beyond this olio of images" to the "young man with dark hair / And uneven eyes, a young man / Leaning on a cane with promises / To keep," the young man who is an authentic image of self. It's not enough to save him, but he learns, momentarily, "still another awful truth: / . . . / *Art saves as often as it kills.*"

Dillard's "The Mullins Farm" raises personal history to fable as the beautiful and terrifying elements of rural chores blend into an extended allegory of survival. The speaker's companion is given "a turtle's heart / Beating, beating in [his] open hand," to hold while its "parts [are] laid out by the fire." This same companion, later, holds a "red hen" that is "soft / And warm as the smell of feathers." Far beyond the didacticism of many "pastoral" poems, "The Mullins Farm" offers no resolution of these seeming oppositions; the evening finds the hounds, surely hunting dogs, "asleep on the front porch, / Their flat brown ears and sharp ribs, / While the cats climb to eat on a fence post." The oaks, however, "rattle acorns in the grass" and "the corn stalks crack in the air," promising re-creation and growth as forceful as any carnivore's hunger.

Many poets born in Virginia have left the state to make their writing careers in other parts of the country. Ellen Bryant Voigt, though born in Chatham, has long made her home in Vermont. Still, her work reflects the interest in rural matters and people that characterizes much southern poetry, and she is perhaps one of the best contemporary examples of the strong historical and aesthetic connections between southern and New England poets. The "Farm Wife," standing in the kitchen in "her long white / gloves of flour," is as fertile as the fields: her "belly / is rising, her apron fills like a sail." This fertility, however, is neither simple nor bucolic; the poem petitions for her freedom, asking for her to be allowed to "float / like a fat gull that swoops and circles" before she is overwhelmed by the demands of family, religion, and "the earth [that] seals / its black mouth like a scar" over her. Though clearly in the tradition of many southern writers, as well as Robert Frost, "Farm Wife" is the poem of a contemporary writer, merciless in her uncovering of the horrors—especially for women—lurking just beneath the beauties of farm life.

Henry Taylor, born in Loudoun County, has recently moved to Maryland and spends much of the year teaching in Washington, D.C. He, too, has devoted much of his writing to the country life of his childhood Virginia. "The Hayfork" returns the speaker to "the old barn floor" where he might still see the "two holes I saw made there," the remaining signs of the "innocent thoughtlessness" that almost killed Joe Trammel. The obsolete hayfork, tripped and dropped by one man who "took a notion" to do it, becomes the imposition of past on present, of danger on the comforting, productive work of baling; and for the speaker, remembering from years later, it becomes the sign of "the way things can go / for years without happening, biding their time." But they do inevitably happen, as surprising and unpredictable in nature as the "quiet whirlwind" in "At South Fork Cemetery" that brings a vivid reminder of spirit to the place where "we stood / cleaning up an overgrown burial ground." Almost a blessing, the "quirk of air" gains meaning when people take it "as something given" from a "thoughtless world" that can also be unexpectedly "generous." More generous, perhaps, than the human social world of "Artichoke," in which a couple reflect differently on the meaning of the sophisticated vegetable. She makes a "predictable remark / about the sensuality of this act," while he wonders "what mind, what hunger, first saw this as food." The poem makes a wry link between the urban and rural spheres that contend for meaning not only in the South but all over turn-of-the-millennium America.

The list of Virginia poets who have made their adult lives and careers outside the state is long, but we claim them as our own, as their roots in the cities and mountains here find their final branching in poems as various as Sally Keith's "The Hunters," tracing the path of one man's attempt to find beautiful patterns in an essentially violent world, where "Death is the pebble . . . slipped from the bridge," and Dana Littlepage Smith's "Asherah," desiring to "grow lean & light" in devotion to Christ. Dave Smith in Maryland (via Louisiana), Molly Bendall in California, Margaret Gibson in Connecticut, John Haines in Montana (via Alaska), David Huddle in Vermont: Virginia-born poets spread the word in all corners of the United States.

The list of those who have come from elsewhere to live and work in Virginia, however, is even longer. The thriving of creative writing programs in many Virginia colleges and universities is surely one reason so many poets have moved to the state. The University of Virginia alone is the professional home of Rita Dove, Charles Wright, Steve Cushman, Lisa Russ Spaar, Gregory Orr, and Debra Nystrom. Hollins has attracted Jeanne Larsen, originally from Washington, D.C., and Eric Trethewey, who was born in Nova Scotia. Washington and Lee University boasts North Carolinian Heather Ross Miller, and Washington, D.C., native Katherine Soniat is one of the creators of a new master's program in writing at Virginia Tech. Even this short list makes clear that the colleges and universities of Virginia have drawn an astonishing number and variety of poets to the area in the last twenty-five years, and these poets have, in turn, educated a significant number of students who have established writing reputations of their own.

This diversity of poets is reflected in the varieties of "Virginia poetry." Rita Dove's narratives in *Thomas and Beulah* dramatize the deceptively simple incremental details that make up the explosive lives she records. "Taking in Wash" operates from a double-vision point of view; the narrative, recalling Theodore Roethke's "My Papa's Waltz," unfolds from a small girl's and an adult's perspective simultaneously. The poem seems governed by the girl's eye: the father arrives home drunk and calls his daughter by her pet name, "Pearl," reminding her that she is, at least sometimes, "Papa's girl, / black though she was." Other details, however—the dog, "a spoiled and ornery bitch," crawling "under the stove" and the mother hiding the laundry—can come only from an older viewer. The tensions finally explode when the father turns to the child, "his smile sliding all over," and the mother responds, *"Touch that child / and I'll cut you down / just like the cedar of Lebanon,"* and the two points of view deftly and dramatically fuse.

Charles Wright's meditative lyrics, often governed by a self-reflective narrator, radically merge colloquial and formal speech, personal and public stances, self-revelatory and self-effacing strategies. "Clear Night" progresses by means of anaphora; the second stanza is a list of Donnean desires, from "I want to be bruised by God" to "I want to be entered and picked clean." It seems a private poem until the final stanza, when the deceptively Romantic speaker, who feels "the wind says 'What?' to me," disappears into the mechanism of the universe, "And the stars start out on their cold slide through the dark. / And the gears notch and the engines wheel." "A Bad Memory Makes You a Metaphysician, A Good One Makes You a Saint" begins, as many Wright poems do, in the backyard of any middle-class American: "This is our world, high privet hedge on two sides, / half-circle of arborvitae, / Small strip of sloped lawn, / Last of the spring tulips and off-purple garlic heads." What could possibly happen in such a manicured world? As it turns out, plenty. The "[d]warf orchard down deep at the bottom of things" is suddenly "God's crucible," and though the neighborhood is "[b]ourgeois, heartbreakingly suburban," it isn't far from "another life," where "the would-be-saints are slipping their hair shirts on." That easily recognizable, quotidian domestic world, like the other "life" that is just as real, is revealed as a linguistic construct, but in fact, there's no other option for us speaking creatures. "Too many things are not left unsaid," the poem ends. "If you want what the syllables want, just do your job." Not a poet of closure, Wright often leaves his poems in a tensive balance. "There is an order beyond form," the speaker says in "Freezing Rain," "but not there. Not here, either."

Within the spectrum of which Dove and Wright might be said to mark the boundaries, the formal and modal ranges in the poetics of Virginia writers are remarkably wide. George Garrett, professor emeritus at the University of Virginia, takes on the faults and foibles of contemporary culture in poems that recall the tradition of English verse satire, both personal and political. "Figure of Speech," launched by a student's malapropism, "It's a doggie dog world," finds the canine metaphor appropriate for a study of the speaker's aging self; his "litter of wounds," once "obedient and gentle," has become "a gaunt and feral pack." The poem moves quickly from mocking to sardonic to dead serious as the speaker grows to understand his woundedness as self-pity: "See their red eyes, / how the hair stands up as they turn against / each other, killing for my choicest parts." "Main Currents of American Political Thought" skewers our received history of presidential greatness, from "(not King no never) George" to "a spoiled country boy / with bad temper and unquenchable appetites." The speaker ends with an unexpected turn to popular culture: "was the man behind the curtain, any of the above, every truly a wizard?"

Nikki Giovanni's sensuous autobiographical lyrics move beyond the simply personal to the emblematic. Speaking with the authority of witness, she celebrates "Knoxville, Tennessee," where she remembers the comfort of a life where body and soul are inseparable. Food—"fresh corn / . . . / and okra / and greens / and cabbage / . . . / and homemade ice-cream"—is best at the "church picnic," and she nostalgically remembers "gospel music / outside / at the church / homecoming."

Given Virginia's deep involvement in America's Revolutionary and Civil Wars, the number of Virginia poets who have been drawn to write about historical subjects is not surprising. The Civil War narratives of Connecticut-born Stephen Cushman recall the work of native Virginian Dave Smith. In Cushman's "View from Lee's Camp," the third-person narrative of memory bleeds into lyric as an aging soldier confronts his approaching death. Having ordered a commemorative plaque and granite "from up north," he's prepared to die: "when he speaks of dying, if he does, / in shrugging off names he cannot remember, / it sounds as though he fears it now / somewhat less, now that he can't wholly take / what little he knows to oblivion with him."

Dave Smith's "On a Field Trip at Fredericksburg" begins with the more immediate frame of first-person, present-tense narrative, but the perspective could scarcely be less private. The setting, the battlefield become tourist site, seems the locus of forgetting rather than memory: "No word / of either Whitman or one uncle / I barely remember." This narrator, however, evokes the "fifteen thousand [who] got it here" in an act that seems almost reverse-synecdoche: "If each finger were a thousand of them / I could clap my hands and be dead / up to my wrists." This gesture initiates the poem's tumble from the Civil War toward "now," when thousands can be killed "quick" with "one bomb, atomic or worse." The poem, now governed not by historical chronology but by association, recalls World War II—"Hiroshima canned nine times their number / in a flash"—even as the narrator stands "above Marye's Heights," where his vision of "Brady's fifteen-year-old / drummers" gives way to the thought that "the names / of birds would gush" if "Audubon came here." The number of deaths in the poem has become staggering, but they devolve on "a wandering child" whom the "[h]opeless teacher" tries, at the end, to guide toward understanding of "a drift of wind / at the forehead, the front door, / the black, numb fingernails."

Henry Hart's meditative "Pocahontas in Jamestown" and his dramatic monologue "Notes from Mount Vernon" challenge historical-site-marker views of America's founding, from the statue of Pocahontas, in "buckskin fringe she never wore," to the "weathervane dove" at Mount Vernon carrying its "olive twig." Lucinda Roy's narratives dramatize Virginia's slave-holding past with horrifying detail. "The Curtsy" tells the fragmentary story of Anna, whose "curtsy was a kind of defecation." Her resistance to the dehumanization of slavery "wasn't mannerly. / It made pale women light up with fury." This understatement makes the punishment, "they lopped off her ears," all the more shocking, but Anna refuses to submit: "she still imbued her curtsies with a curse." The men's best strategy for regaining control is rhetorical—"Old Ellis" praises her baking, then tells the men, " 'These biscuits slip down your throat like the tongue of a whore' "— but no less revolting. The other men "nod, knowing precisely what he meant." In "The Virginia Reel," the plantation is now, like so many antebellum sites, a tourist stop, and the "slave quarters are full / of whimsy." The title suggests that a celebration of southern culture is in the offing, and the guide is certainly overwhelmed with admiration for the wealthy trappings of the house. The narrator, however, is able see a different past in the story of the apparent apotheosis of a slave, appropriately named Elijah. This astonishing tale of spiritual yearning and final escape—"He flew!"—undercuts the more acceptable story of " 'the great quest for harmony' " upon which, at the poem's end, the guide—and the now ironic title—continues to insist.

H. L. Mencken said that it was impossible to find a poet anywhere in the South. It was a questionable contention even in the early twentieth century, and now the number and variety of poets in and from Virginia gives the lie to such a dismissal. The number is so great, in fact, that this volume is limited to living poets who meet the following criteria. First, all have published at least one book with a nationally recognized press. Second, all were born, are currently living, or have spent a significant part of their professional lives in Virginia. Last, all are actively engaged in the creative community of our region. The poets gathered here are authors of some of the best poetry being written anywhere, from the "holy world of words" that Margaret Gibson celebrates in "Earth Elegy" to the murderous dramatic monologue that Steve Scafidi imagines in "To Whoever Set My Truck on Fire." Even those writers who have passed through Virginia and moved on have left their marks on our state, on students and colleagues and friends, adding deeper tones to our already remarkable breadth of voice, style, and subject. In selecting the poems for this anthology, we have discovered not just a distinctive "Virginia voice," but the many Virginias—personal and political, past and present, private and public—that writers who have sojourned here are creating. This collection is not merely a compilation of poems about our corner of the nation but is a rich cross-section of the lyrics and narratives, the meditations and satires, the autobiographical and historical explorations that, together, make up contemporary American verse.

Common Wealth

Talvikki Ansel

Winner of the 1996 Yale Younger Poets Prize for
My Shining Archipelago, *Talvikki Ansel earned
her A.B. at Mount Holyoke College and her M.F.A.
at Indiana University. Ms. Ansel has also received
a Wallace Stegner fellowship and a Virginia
Commission for the Arts grant. Her work has
appeared in the* Atlantic Monthly, *the* New
Republic, *the* Indiana Review, *and the Pushcart
Prize anthology. She recently taught at Virginia
Commonwealth University in Richmond.*

John Clare

Spondee; name—
damp earth and distance. This
is what it's like to leave—first
the dirt, robin perched
on the handle of the spade; Mary, up-
ending a bucket for him to sit
while she hisses the milk into a pail,
ear pressed to a flank, lap,
the fern owl's nest. Enclosure, 1810—
the first act, the moors
all cut like quilt nap. Blue
thread of pain.—Why does *anyone*
think they can step back? (me,
when I close my eyes I
can see the hill beyond
the larch, cows like specks—)
Homesick? Blue flax, birds' eggs,
he writes: the moor, "its only
bondage the circling sky." The blackbird
in the coppice churrs, "we have no name for
burst of spring." Doctor Allen
feels the perfect dome, ellipse—
ellipsis—of his skull; phrenology at Fairmead

House for the Insane; vicissitudes of weather on
the subject's mind. *The Flitting,* "summer
like a stranger comes . . . I envy birds,"
sweeping clear sky. John Clare,
"my life hath been one love," escapes:
wet ditches, Mary, "my life
hath been one chain of contradictions,"
in search of Mary—dead now
three years, eating grass.
And this: when he dies the villagers lift
the lid of the coffin, see if it's
he, keep midnight vigil; keep
at bay a London surgeon wanting
to slice the top of his skull, to study
the tempest settling.

Study Skins

Grit of cornmeal, borax,
the neck droops over my hand,
limp wings. Clean slit
from the cloaca, I peel back
skin from the breast—gently
not to stretch it. How neatly
it all fits together. Flies.
Outside, a blackbird squawks.
                    Rough bumps
of the feather tracts under skin,
each feather a bump. The innards
textbook perfect: gleaming
liver lobes, the heart
clean as a thumb, trachea—
windpipe—fluted hollow
holding the breath. Inside out
the wing's white bone
juts up, the thigh.
My hair falls into my face—so easy

to dig out the skull,
pry out the eyes. Outside,
the air all brightness, warm bayberry:
light, whole and beating. I think
what's to keep
me from dissipating, evaporating,
like a breath
or the blackbird's call?
I make a body from a stick
wrapped in cotton, imbed
it in the skull. My hands
sticky and caught
with pieces of tissue and down,
some in my hair, on my brow.
When I'm done, the guts
a small pile on the newspaper,
the birds, wings folded,
stare straight up to the ceiling.
Eyes filled with cotton,

wide and blank as if
they've seen some mystery
I don't see, whole —*fluted*—
which means furrowed, clear.

4

*A teacher at George Mason University, Jennifer
Atkinson was born in 1955 and received her
education at Wesleyan University and the University
of Iowa. Ms. Atkinson was awarded a Pushcart
Prize for poetry in 1988 and won the Samuel French
Morse Poetry Prize for her collection* The Drowned
City *(Northeastern University 2000). Her first book
of poems,* The Dogwood Tree, *was published in
1990 by the University of Alabama Press. Her
work has also appeared in numerous journals,
including* Field, Poetry, *the* Yale Review, *and
the* New England Review.

The Dogwood Tree

Mown once at midsummer, the field
has taken months to recover
its half-wild hodgepodge of color—
the shades now of early fall.
From the window, she can guess at
what grows there. The purple must
be joe-pye weed, the yellow tufts
would be goldenrod. That red
bush is a blueberry, that blue
spire a cedar. She hasn't
been moved to walk down there all year—
among the briars and broken
stalks—to find the small lives
distance obscures. But in the center
there is a dogwood tree,
as straight and perfectly round
as a child would draw it. The leaves
have gone red, and the berries,
past ripe, are now wine. She can tell
by the birds. A whole flock of

something black—grackles or starlings—
has descended to feast on
the fruit. It happens every year.
And every year the birds fall,
drunken from the hidden branches,
easy, almost willing prey.
This year she would like to touch one,
open its vulnerable
wings in her hands, feel its talons,
its fear, the glare of its black,
yellow-rimmed eye. And she would like
to return the bird unharmed
to the ground where it fell, reeling,
close to what she might call joy.

Sky Shows around the Edges

The leafless trees and the leaf-strewn, ulterior
thawing woods—catbrier, lichen, and the elsewhere-scarce
    candelabra
ground pine—all that and the laurel glassy with rain.

Test that green and the lustrous planes of the hemlock against
the dangled plumb bob of a single word.

Three Years: A Composition in Gesso and Graphite

From the drowned marsh-island lumbers the osprey.

Low inland fog annulled the creek and byways, all
but the tallest, tasseled reeds. Like sleep

mist overtakes rank distance and detail,
near and far, the expanse of wind-

trampled salt hay, the stiff seed crowns
at the creek edge. What dream is this

that your refusal should lie so quiet,
your heart the palm-up concave of a clamshell?

What cold dream that only the osprey, hunting, wakes?

Molly Bendall

Karen Fish

Born in Richmond in 1961, Molly Bendall holds an M.F.A. from the University of Virginia. Ms. Bendall won the Peregrine Smith Poetry Prize in 1992 for her first book, After Estrangement. *She has also received the Eunice Tietjens Prize from* Poetry *magazine, the Lynda Hull Poetry Award from* Denver Quarterly, *and two Pushcart Prizes. Her newest books are* Dark Summer *(1999) and* Ariadne's Island *(2002), both from Miami University Press. Ms. Bendall currently teaches at the University of Southern California and lives in Venice, California.*

A Shade Away

Dear Julian, Won't you remember it, how we'd fling ourselves
into the late, late afternoon? We'd visit the pier, our catwalk
to admire our shadows swinging against the nomad sun,
that come-hithering sun and wait for it to turn
as pink as Schiaparelli's pink. I'd play
my nearly piqued self until the marketplace attracted us, pulled
us in. Try this on. And we'd carry off the pleats with begonias
hidden in the folds. More anthuriums—we might have licked
   their rims.
But then, you always really wanted to live (much more than I)
in the kingdom of nonchalance. That summer, the soaring
length of it . . . I had to fan the air.
I long to put on the clothes you wore and parade around in them.
Our furniture ended up splintered, and you left
in a vase a sorry-wrinkled-note for me with no hidden bridges,
no beckoning loops in the cursive flair.
I kept a few light and tender bruises to match the dusk,
where we treated the sailboats to our mastery.
A toast. *"Très gentil."* Further and everlasting
. . . sails. They've become dancers holding a note in a line
to almost-nowhere. Why do I look on it this way—so relentlessly?
The skirts on the water still shimmer in their own rosy wakes.

Bird Talk

Dear Annette, Let's wrap up in a fox
    who's biting his own
        plume tail,
        and spring being wrecked as it is,
        decorate
the birds on fleurs-de-lys plates.
They asked, "Do you like our
        widows' peaks?" (Oh, their little
walnut heads.)
        Our snaps are undone.
    Where should we go with our fish hook
        lighters?
Our sampler's complete—cross stitch
    satin stitch, French
        twist,
        blanket, needle . . . trim.
It's how we'll go a'nutting, *n'est pas?*
    And fritter away the detail,
        enact our ode to makeup on and on,
until we look like
        tufted puffins.
    For a finale: the birds garnished
        with luminescent-pearl-ends
        of pins.
    Whisper, hush, call it even,
    until we're almost singing.
A bed of thrush holding
        our nesting, erotic selves.
    We'll lull them
        and have more to count
    and less to worry for.
        Our coat and gloves are clean.

(for Annette Messager)

Kelly Cherry

Daaave Summers

*Richmond native Kelly Cherry is the author of five
volumes of poetry from Louisiana State University
Press:* God's Loud Hand, Natural Theology,
Relativity: A Point of View, Lovers and Agnostics,
and Venus Rising. *She has also published five works
of fiction, two of nonfiction, and a translation of
Seneca's* Octavia. *Ms. Cherry served as the Evjue-
Bascom Professor in Humanities and the Eudora
Welty Professor Emerita of English at the University
of Wisconsin and is currently the visiting Eminent
Scholar at the University of Alabama at Huntsville.
She lives on a small farm in Halifax, Virginia.*

On Watching a Young Man Play Tennis

The male poets run, lifting their feet like pros.
Others fish, and then there are those
Whose driving force
Sends them to the sandtraps of an eighteen-hole course

In search of metaphor. I have no yen
For sun and sky and earth, no kin-
Ship for the sea.
The element of mind is quite enough for me,

And dreaming in the damp of poolside shade,
I let imagination wade
Through the shallow
Stretch of time beyond a bend of tanning elbow,

And burning thigh, to where the poet plays
A love game with my yesterdays.
I have no zest
For exercise, no yearning after limberness

For the sake of limb alone, but enjoy,
Girlishly, this energy of Boy
That seeks to know
The meaning of *mens sana in corpore sano.*

Turning on my side, I see the shadow
Of his racket on the court grow
Long and widen
Till its very silence trespasses on the Haydn

Which carries from the house, and I put down
My drink and move inside where sound
And light and drift
Of dinner's smells serve, albeit fleetingly, to lift

My spirits to a plane of praise upon
Which I can stand and frankly own
That I am tired,
And lazy, and will leave to others more inspired

The satisfaction of the outdoor sports.
A young man in his tennis shorts
Suffices to
Realign the balance of my brain and back so

That I am paralyzed with memory
Of verse and versifier. (Yet I
Remember when
I volleyed more than words with the artfullest of men.)

Epithalamium

For my parents' Golden Anniversary, 1983

Although he is still surprised
That it has turned out this way
After all the years when
It seemed it wouldn't,

My father loves my mother
So much that there are times when
He is afraid he is going to die
Of it, the anxiety,

And there are times when
He thinks that would be a relief,
Better than the dis-ease of heart
That awaits him when she goes.

With his arthritic fingers
He threads the needle
She can no longer see
The eye of.

Michael Chitwood

*Michael Chitwood was born in Rocky Mount,
Virginia, in 1958 and educated at Emory and Henry
College and the University of Virginia. His most
recent book of poems,* The Weave Room, *was
published in 1998 by the University of Chicago Press.
He is also the author of* Whet (Ohio Review 1995)
and a collection of essays, Hitting below the Bible
Belt *(Down Home 1998). Mr. Chitwood has been
awarded a Poets and Writers' Exchange Award and
an individual arts grant from the North Carolina
Arts Council. He is currently a visiting lecturer at the
University of North Carolina at Chapel Hill.*

Thinking of Rome in Fair Lea, West Virginia

Help me remember,
I wanted to say to the man wrestling the drag chain
onto the back of the fair's largest John Deere,
what is the name of the church that holds
St. Peter's bones and a bit of the chain
in which he was brought to Rome.
This thing could drag a whale from the deep
if you could find a way to hook him up, he said.
Of the man shouting about elephant rides, tigers and the rare
     black leopard,
I wanted to ask what entrance
the emperors used to process into the coliseum
and how many gates sorted the people of Rome into their seats.
You will see amazing feats, he said:
men consumed in flame and yet not burned.
The man with the "Kill'em All Let God Sort'em Out" tee shirt
said nothing but pulled the lever
and set the neon bones of the Ferris wheel whirling,
rattling above the souls along the midway
like link chain jangling on the ankles of the vanquished.

Weave Room

Because the room roared,
two hundred Draper looms
throttled to make the most
of extra-yard bonus,
and because they made
the machines sing until
they carried deafness
home like an empty
lunch box,
they mastered a speech
held in hands.
I've seen fights begin
from the way one
took hold of another
to move him away
from a breakdown.
Gossip traveled
on fingertips.
But best of all
was the semaphore
they invented
with the flashlights
they used to understand
the greased hearts of looms.
Hanging in thongs,
voices potent as the rock
in David's sling.
They spoke across
the scream of the room,
shot the air
with syllables of light.

Rosanne Coggeshall

Born in 1946 in Florence, South Carolina, Rosanne Coggeshall earned her B.A. and M.A. from Hollins College and lived for many years in Daleville and Fincastle, Virginia. Ms. Coggeshall has published three volumes of poetry from Louisiana State University Press: Hymn for Drum, Traffic with Ghosts, *and* Fire or Fire. *She is now retired and at work on a novella in Pittsboro, North Carolina.*

Jets

Tell me about jet rags.
Tell me about the vertical daggers
in the road all pointing north.
Tell me about Moon Pies & Cokes
you buy conveniently as you drive,
jokes men toss at you
through windows like soiled socks.

Say you are twenty:
you leave the house alone at dusk,
crank up the engine to sail sunset back
to *your* state now, Virginia, New York,
or Maryland—it makes all of the difference.
When you hit the road to Gretna
you change your mind:
you flip the switch,
cut cruise control, decide:
you'll stay at the Greenwood,
Route 315, have some fried chicken,
some turnip greens and a cup or two of joe,
one to go so that you can slip into the night
& walk that deep hill to the place where the counties
split and the country roils and rambles
like a feverish dream.

That coffee will slosh
but that's fine: all will be well,
all manner of thing shall be well
and you'll wake earlier than the sun
and run down Route 315 as far as you can,
until you see a farmer pitching hay—
there will be new calves in the meadow,
corn in the crib.

You'll know, somehow,
you'll run that route
as long as it takes
to make the byways safe
for every mad dog, every hen.

Prayer for the Whole State

All Saints' Day

Under cover, volcanic and alone,
you rivet rage to sun straps
as they bind the room.
It is never earlier, never later
than the heart's bell sprung,
wrung.

Grievous everywhere, small people rant and hide.
The world's acrostics break.
Each of several continents divides.
Women lead babies, hungry, eyes wide;
fathers vie and vie and vie
into night perpetual
until little people die:
they don't get up.

Stiff strife in cleated shoes
stalks mightier and full.

Any hour and all at once
merriment and murder sear, astound.
Famine blasts. Fire and ornament expound.

And somewhere, in the distance,
all around a yew tree,
servants gather on their knees.
The bartered tree lights higher.
There are meadows in the breeze.

Stephen Cushman

*Educated at Cornell and Yale Universities, Stephen
Cushman, born in 1956, has been a professor of
American literature and poetry at the University of
Virginia since 1982. He has published two volumes
of poetry,* Cussing Lesson *(2002) and* Blue Pajamas
*(1998), both from Louisiana State University Press.
Mr. Cushman is also the author of two books of
criticism,* Fictions of Form in American Poetry
(Princeton University 1993) and William Carlos
Williams and the Meanings of Measure *(Yale
University 1985). He is an advisory editor for the*
Virginia Quarterly Review.

View from Lee's Camp

White-haired now, he played as a boy
where the fireplace bricks still stood
and piles of stones that supported the floor
still described the shape of the tent
before bulldozer blades had swept them away,
before the cherry tree where they must have tied
the famous horse came down, before each playmate
died in turn and left him alone, the only one
living who knew where it was. At the funeral home
he ordered granite from up north, along with a plaque
to mark the spot, the hillock on a treeless hip
of the final mountain between Orange and the sea
a perfect place to watch the plank road from,
the traffic there rattling off to the Wilderness,
or to focus farther off and see, if not quite Richmond,
sixty miles southeast, beyond the geese
rising in formation, then at least what Richmond
needed to be told. *Unless there is a change, I fear
the army cannot be kept effective.* When he speaks
of war, he almost makes it sound like *woe,*
and when he speaks of dying, if he does,

in shrugging off names he cannot remember,
it sounds as though he fears it now
somewhat less, now that he can't wholly take
what little he knows to oblivion with him.

Second Opinion

Erat illimis fons. "There was a clear spring"
doesn't quite get it, the sense of slimelessness
Ovid wanted, and let's ease up on Narcissus.
Imagine how it feels to have your name twisted

into a term that's never a compliment.
Okay, he's good looking, a little stuck up,
but why plunge overboard on sympathy for Echo—
she got hers for hoodwinking Juno—and before you go

slapping his name on somebody else, make sure
you read the damn story: *Quod petis est nusquam.*
"What you seek is nowhere": wound beyond balm.
And all because Narcissus said no

to someone who bitched to Nemesis.
Where would we be if everybody's id
could revenge itself on the unrequiting,
and what about empathy for the cursed kid

suddenly burning in his own blind fire?
Disorders need naming, though, let's be fair,
and who can blame Näcke or Ellis or Freud
that the beautiful boy forgot himself fully

when he fell for his face and having kissed
tasteless water only then realized
the terrible error. That part doesn't fit;
yet it's not the fault of your local therapist,

who's making a living and may not wonder
why the gods would change a loser
bad enough to name our problems after
into white flowers with a saffron center.

Julia Johnson

Richard Dillard

*Richard Dillard, born in Roanoke in 1937, teaches
English and heads the creative writing department
at Hollins University, where he also edits the* Hollins
Critic. *He has published five volumes of poetry from
Louisiana State University Press, including* Sallies;
Just Here, Just Now; *and* News of the Nile, *as well
as two novels and two books of criticism. In 1994,
he won the O. B. Hardison Jr. Poetry Prize given by
the Folger Shakespeare Library. His work has also
appeared in* Chronicles, Denver Quarterly, *and*
Quarterly West.

Poe at the End

October. Poe in Baltimore. Poe
At the end, going North, away
From Virginia, keeping promises
Despite the black beak of despair,
Laid over, waiting for the train,
But just now, drunk, out of the coop,
Leaning in Lombard Street
Against the window of a store,
Making his pitched and stammered way
Toward Cooth & Sergeant's Tavern—
(Sergeant Major Poe, First Artillery,
Honorably discharged so many years ago)—
Slow way of starts and fits,
The drink and drugs sluing his heart
Into blind staggers and sways.

Away from Virginia and toward
Virginia in the grave. She played
The harp that January night and sang,
It was a good song, too,
But so soon, so quickly a tiny vessel
Popped in her throat like a New Year's squib

Just as she reached for her last high note.
And for five years it broke and broke
Again, until she died, was laid away,
And Poe learned an awful truth:
Helter skelter or catcher in the rye,
Art kills as often as it saves.

On Lombard Street in Baltimore, memory
Twists him, presses his forehead against the glass,
His heart wheezing like wind through the cottage wall
In Fordham where Virginia lay. His heart lifts
In his chest, flaps clumsily aloft
Like a great white bird, then settles back,
And Poe is grounded, left in the lurch
As he was abandoned by his party friends
After voting all morning under a dozen names:
His own, Usher, Reynolds, Dupin, Pym,
Raising his hand again and again, taking the oath,
Swearing he was who he was and was not,
Swearing he was.
                                    Hart Crane asked him
Nearly a century later whether he denied
The ticket, but how could he deny a thing,
He who was all things that day and none,
A multitude of beings and only one,
Leaning on a window, his forehead on the glass,
His eyes unfocused or focused deep within.

And yet he does see past Virginia
With blood on her blouse, past Elmira
Left behind in Richmond, jilted
Before she ever reached the altar,
Past even the bloated face of Edgar Poe
Reflected in the window, drawn and drawn out
In the wobbly glass, the sodden man
In a stranger's threadbare clothes
With only Dr. Carter's borrowed cane
Still clutched in that familiar hand,

Sees through the tortured glass
To a display of pewter and silver
Laid out within the shop, slick knives
With thin images of a singular man
Upon each blade, rounded shining cups
With a bulge-nosed alien face
In each curved surface, two large
Silver plates with his own desperate stare
Reflected plain in each, the brow,
The carved-out cheeks, blue lips
Beneath the sad mustache.
        But he
Looks beyond this olio of images,
These hard lies and harder truths
Displayed before him, to find
A large silver coffee urn, beknobbed
And crusted with handles and thick
Vines, blossoms and twisted ribbons,
Its surface flat and curved and rounded,
Concave, convex, and convolute,
And in its turbulent reflections
He sees a young man's face,
A young man with dark hair
And uneven eyes, a young man
Leaning on a cane with promises
To keep, a face he recognizes
But cannot name, knows but cannot claim,
That looks him steadily eye to eye.

His heart will soon calm down enough
For him to stutter on, reach Cooth &
Sergeant's, fall onto a bench, be found,
Be carried to the hospital, lie there in fever,
Call Reynolds' name, ease out of delirium
Only to say, gently, "Lord help my poor soul,"
And die, having for one moment on Lombard Street
Learned still another awful truth:

Pell mell or waiting just to die,
Art saves as often as it kills.

The Mullins Farm

The sun through the window
Is as warm as the smell of salt,
Of hams, the hum of bees
Where the smoke bellows lie
On the table by the netting,
The hat and the gloves.

My uncle hands you a turtle's heart,
Beating, beating in your open hand,
His head still hooked on the broom,
The hollow of his bones on the ground,
And his parts laid out by the fire,
The kettle made ready for soup.

The high horse, Mack, dappled white,
And the brown, too, slow and full,
The hill that falls off from the barn
Where the corn is husked in the dark,
And the hogs hanging to be split,
Filled with apples and corn and sweet slop.

By the branch out back and the small bridge,
In the damp concrete walls, the milk
Sits in spring water, and the squares
Of pressed butter, each with its bouquet
Of spring flowers, and on the bank,
An occasional frog or small snake.

The horseshoes must be bent on hot coals,
Red and white as new flowers, sprinkled
On the ground around the anvil, inviting

To your hand which must never touch,
And the shadows of the waiting horses,
The hot hammers, the hard men.

The red hen in your arms is soft
And warm as the smell of feathers,
As the afternoon, while a small hawk
Watches from a crooked pine, watches
My grandfather in his clean tan clothes
Load his shotgun in the porch's shade.

And my grandmother rings the wood stove,
Takes the biscuits from the high warmer,
Calls her daughters to set the table.
And feeds the large family with squirrel
And green beans, squash and mashed potatoes
As a brace of dead crows hang from the fence.

The afternoon is unending and clear
As the branches in front of and behind
The white house, as you climb the hill
To the barn, smell the stacked hay,
Touch the smooth wood of the stalls,
And see the sun powdered by barn dust.

My grandfather has cut a log of green wood
And set it up in the fireplace
With dry props to light as the evening
Comes on, and you may sit in the dim room
With the shadows wrinkling your face,
Hear the fire living in the light's slow leak.

The hounds are asleep on the front porch,
Their flat brown ears and sharp ribs,
While the cats climb to eat on a fence post,
And the oaks rattle acorns in the grass
And on the tin roof of the porch,
And the corn stalks crack in the air.

Gregory Donovan

T. R. Hummer

Gregory Donovan is an associate professor of English and the director of creative writing at Virginia Commonwealth University in Richmond. Born in 1950 in Arkansas, he won the 1993 Devins Award for Poetry from the University of Missouri Press for Calling His Children Home *and has received a fellowship in poetry from the Virginia Commission for the Arts. His work has been published in the* Kenyon Review, New England Review, *and the* Southern Review.

25

The Grandfather in the Rafters

A form of revenge. Some homegrown Missouri craftsman here
    committed
a bridge. Now it rots under its caved-in, cedar-shingled cover
where once it leapt with a certain grace, windowed, gabled, fitted
true as any man's good house, right as rain, clean over

that small island of brush in the raw-banked, often-as-not dry
branch. Where, you said, one summer's day you hid
to watch the goddamn stiff-neck dandy take his ride
through the tall noon. His mare's mane of shining amber

whipping back. His boiled and studded shirtfront, never
stained by anything like sweat. A man's ramrod
straight and lordly, until he slowed her to enter—
hoof-clops and wheels rumbling overhead in the lumber—

the shadow in the bridge. In that dark mouth he had been
a thundering brag, a half-minute's worth of hollow
promises, empty threats. And when he came to light again
you spit in your palm. Then smiled. You'd call his bluff.

He went courting every woman a young man might desire
for miles around in that expensive, trim, and pillowed

rig, the black calash top always thrown back
to show off the seat's tan soft-soaped leathers. Your rough

farm-boy hands were itching for just the truck
a swill bucket full of slop and black mud might do.
So you sneaked back to climb where you waited, eyes afire
with the framed spark of stars, to throw down that night

a county baptism and burial, a handful of hard words
through gritted teeth: *Here you go, Mister Man: you're dirt, too.*
But he raised up when the horse spooked, and you heard
the thump of his fall making you dead right.

Runes

He is walking in a logically foreign country
in a locale open to scouring wind and sun
which has offered its perfected face
to the light thrust of many ancient stars
and masks of moons, disfigured as the guileless
blank look of a loving woman he has betrayed.

He stops to pick up a stone, reads
chipped there a fragment of the indecipherable
letter, and haunted with the carver's presence
he looks over his shoulder, checks his bearings, wanting
eventually to return, though he understands
he will not, there will be no need:

The place has known him fully as the one
who would come wandering and distracted
to the grounded shard and know himself
as the one to leave it there again misplaced,
another shift in the always human landscape,
the ruined word, the old power, touched, revenant.

Rita Dove

*Born in 1952 in Akron, Ohio, Rita Dove is
Commonwealth Professor of English at the University
of Virginia. She is the author of six books of poems,
including* Thomas and Beulah *(Carnegie Mellon
University 1986), which was awarded the 1987
Pulitzer Prize;* On the Bus with Rosa Parks *(Norton
1999);* Selected Poems *(Vintage 1993); and* Grace
Notes *(Norton 1989). She has received Fulbright,
Guggenheim, and Mellon fellowships, as well as the
Levinson Prize from* Poetry. *Ms. Dove has also
written a novel, a book of stories, a verse drama, a
collection of essays, and the song cycle "Seven for
Luck." She served as poet laureate of the United
States from 1993 to 1995.*

Parsley

1. *The Cane Fields*

There is a parrot imitating spring
in the palace, its feathers parsley green.
Out of the swamp the cane appears

to haunt us, and we cut it down. El General
searches for a word; he is all the world
there is. Like a parrot imitating spring,

we lie down screaming as rain punches through
and we come up green. We cannot speak an R—
out of the swamp, the cane appears

and then the mountain we call in whispers *Katalina.*
The children gnaw their teeth to arrowheads.
There is a parrot imitating spring.

El General has found his word: *perejil.*
Who says it, lives. He laughs, teeth shining
out of the swamp. The cane appears

in our dreams, lashed by wind and streaming.
And we lie down. For every drop of blood
there is a parrot imitating spring.
Out of the swamp the cane appears.

2.   *The Palace*

The word the general's chosen is parsley.
It is fall, when thoughts turn
to love and death; the general thinks
of his mother, how she died in the fall
and he planted her walking cane at the grave
and it flowered, each spring stolidly forming
four-star blossoms. The general
pulls on his boots, he stomps to
her room in the palace, the one without
curtains, the one with a parrot
in a brass ring. As he paces he wonders
Who can I kill today. And for a moment
the little knot of screams
is still. The parrot, who has traveled

all the way from Australia in an ivory
cage, is, coy as a widow, practicing
spring. Ever since the morning
his mother collapsed in the kitchen
while baking skull-shaped candies
for the Day of the Dead, the general
has hated sweets. He orders pastries
brought up for the bird; they arrive

dusted with sugar on a bed of lace.
The knot in his throat starts to twitch;

he sees his boots the first day in battle
splashed with mud and urine
as a soldier falls at his feet amazed—
how stupid he looked!—at the sound
of artillery. *I never thought it would sing*
the soldier said, and died. Now

the general sees the fields of sugar
cane, lashed by rain and streaming.
He sees his mother's smile, the teeth
gnawed to arrowheads. He hears
the Haitians sing without R's
as they swing the great machetes:
Katalina, they sing, *Katalina*,

mi madle, mi amol en muelte. God knows
his mother was no stupid woman; she
could roll an R like a queen. Even
a parrot can roll an R! In the bare room
the bright feathers arch in a parody
of greenery, as the last pale crumbs
disappear under the blackened tongue. Someone

calls out his name in a voice
so like his mother's, a startled tear
splashes the tip of his right boot.
My mother, my love in death.
The general remembers the tiny green sprigs
men of his village wore in their capes
to honor the birth of a son. He will
order many, this time, to be killed

for a single, beautiful word.

The Event

Ever since they'd left the Tennessee ridge
with nothing to boast of
but good looks and a mandolin,

the two Negroes leaning
on the rail of a riverboat
were inseparable: Lem plucked

to Thomas' silver falsetto.
But the night was hot and they were drunk.
They spat where the wheel

churned mud and moonlight,
they called to the tarantulas
down among the bananas

to come out and dance.
You're so fine and mighty; let's see
what you can do, said Thomas, pointing

to a tree-capped island.
Lem stripped, spoke easy: *Them's chestnuts,*
I believe. Dove

quick as a gasp. Thomas, dry
on deck, saw the green crown shake
as the island slipped

under, dissolved
in the thickening stream.
At his feet

a stinking circle of rags,
the half-shell mandolin.
Where the wheel turned the water

gently shirred.

Taking in Wash

Papa called her Pearl when he came home
drunk, swaying as if the wind touched
only him. Towards winter his skin paled,
buckeye to ginger root, cold drawing
the yellow out. The Cherokee in him,
Mama said. Mama never changed:
when the dog crawled under the stove
and the back gate slammed, Mama hid
the laundry. Sheba barked as she barked
in snow or clover, a spoiled and ornery bitch.

She was Papa's girl,
black though she was. Once,
in winter, she walked through a dream
all the way down the stairs
to stop at the mirror, a beast
with stricken eyes
who screamed the house awake. Tonight

every light hums, the kitchen arctic
with sheets. Papa is making the hankies
sail. Her foot upon a silk
stitched rose, she waits
until he turns, his smile sliding all over.
Mama a tight dark fist.
Touch that child

and I'll cut you down
just like the cedar of Lebanon.

Canary

for Michael S. Harper

Billie Holiday's burned voice
had as many shadows as lights,
a mournful candelabra against a sleek piano,
the gardenia her signature under that ruined face.

(Now you're cooking, drummer to bass,
magic spoon, magic needle.
Take all day if you have to
with your mirror and your bracelet of song.)

Fact is, the invention of women under siege
has been to sharpen love in the service of myth.

If you can't be free, be a mystery.

Kent Ippolito

Claudia Emerson

*Claudia Emerson is an associate professor of English
at Mary Washington College and a contributing
editor to* Shenandoah. *Born in Chatham, Virginia,
in 1957, she received her education at the University
of Virginia and the University of North Carolina—
Greensboro, where she was poetry editor of the*
Greensboro Review. *She has been a visiting
professor at Washington and Lee University and has
received fellowships from the National Endowment
for the Arts and the Virginia Commission for the
Arts. Her books are* Pinion: An Elegy *(2002) and*
Pharaoh, Pharaoh *(1997), both from Louisiana
State University Press.*

Auction

Some things bring nothing. Later there will be
a bonfire of palm-worn plow handles.
But a doll, pallid—china hands fractured—
brings fifteen dollars.
          His bed they have hauled
out, the covers still on it, an old man's
nest of tangled flannel. I think he has
no daughters to know what must not be
sold. His late wife's dressing table gives up
its confused vanities: snaggletooth combs,
the warbled wire of hairpins, a lipstick,
a faint layer of blush over all. The sun-
shocked mirror denies this face, waves my hair,
widens my eyes until I cannot see
the resemblance. Is this how she saw
herself? And over her shoulder the fields,
falling away from the house, steep with
distortion? Under her crushed narcissus,
the varicose wake of a mole heaves

as if the vagrant dead—grown bolder—rise,
thick palms bared for this shallow, movable darkness.

Plagues

A rain crow lusts in the hot, waxy pines.
Day after day a red-tail thirsts against
the flat sky: the field mice dry and dying,
there is nothing worth leaving the thermals.
Tobacco burns in the fields, and corn
smothers in its silk. The cows, blowsy, slow,
brood in the sallow pond, hooves sunk, sucking
silky mud that rises like blood.
                                        "Smitten,
we are smitten with old plagues." The great-aunt
waves her hands, her thin forearms sumac-red
with easy bruises.
                        "Aw, listen to you,"
I humor her, "we are having a drought,
but the almanac—"
                        "—did not predict these
seventeen-year locusts." She's mad now. "'Pharaoh,
Pharaoh,' hear them plead?"
                                        I listen, but hear
wordless their persistent rumor. "I don't know
about that, Aunt Kate; I don't remember
the Bible like you do."
                        "I would tear out
your tongue like a bloody root," she tells me,
"but I am tired," lays down her head in her
narrow lap. A hymn trembles, rises from
her thighs: *Shall we gather at the river?*

The neighbor cranks the '49 Ford motor
that runs his irrigation pump, faithless:
the fields shoulder the rank beat of wings, wings
of bitter water. All night the orphaned

locusts wheeze in the darkness, grafted now
with disinherited language, until
we are all of one mind, one swollen tongue:
Pharaoh, Pharaoh, as if there were something
keeping us, as if we could be let go.

The Taxidermist

In good weather I herd them onto my lawn,
coats glossy, feathers bold. Cars slow for the fox
beside the quail, the bobcat by the sleeping
fawn. I turned each body inside out,
emptied it of flesh, fat, bone, eyes; the meat
of the lie displays the thin defining skin
of something else. All that you see, I save.
Good enough to shoot again, you laugh,
but I know death is not held at bay, has not
even looked over its shoulder at the fleshing knives
and pliers, the saws and scalpels. This is tedious,
messy resurrection, and what I preserve
is not death or life or skill but the wounded
ghost of an old hunger that won't be tamed
and taught to lick your hand, old hunter, but will
bound through some finer field, beyond the wind
you foul, even as I rummage for the right
glass eye in drawered compartments. Here, see,
they are all here: loon, lynx, buck, fox, quail,
snake, and coon. All measured, all perfect, all blind.

The Admirer

September, 1926, clear

He had before come courting—with pecans
or peaches, berries. She had those times been able

to thank him with one of her pies and be
done with him. For this, though, he would want
supper, to sit at the table with her
after supper. For this, she reckoned he had
spent most of the morning emptying
the sky of its plenty: the doves spilled from
burlap in iridescent disarray,
three dozen at least, a shimmering

bouquet. And so the afternoon was for her
defined; the hour deepened the mound of feathers,
blue-gray, plucked in porch-dusk, and the wind,
disinterested, would once in a while stir them.
She knew they were easy to bring down
over a field where they would fall into
the tangled grasses and go on flying against
what had been wind. Easy—as this was not:
feet, gut, heart, the smooth brow with eyes open
like garnets glowing; she cut and tossed over

and over what was in the end useless
onto the feathers, a last and bloody bed,
or to the cats, who growled and circled her,
to keep the peace. A dove would amount to,
at best, a half-dozen mouthfuls, the dark
breast tender but gristled with shot—black seed.
She threw a whole bird to the nursing cat
and wondered whether the white kitten had opened
its eyes; if they were blue, it would be deaf,
she had been told and told she could not let it

live. She would see about that. Her mother called down
how are they coming. More work than they're worth,
she answered back, for such a little meat.
Even with the birds still baking, yet to be
eaten, with still the biscuits to stir up
and gravy yet to make from the meager fat—

with a strait hour to pass before he would
lean back from the table to pick his teeth and sigh—
she had decided he should have left the doves
their beloved sky, for she would not be won.

C. D. Wright

Forrest Gander

Forrest Gander, born in 1956 in Barstow, California, and raised in northern Virginia, is the director of the writing program at Brown University. Mr. Gander's two most recent collections of poetry are Torn Awake *(2001) and* Science and Steepleflower *(1998), both from New Directions Press. He has received a National Endowment for the Arts fellowship in poetry, a Whiting Award for Writers, and a Gertrude Stein Award for Innovative Writing. His work has appeared in* Denver Quarterly, American Poetry Review, *and the* Southern Review.

Field Guide to Southern Virginia

True as the circumference
to its center. Woodscreek Grocery,
Rockbridge County. Twin boys
peer from the front window, cheeks
bulging with fireballs. Sandplum trees
flower in clusters by the levee. She
makes a knot on the inside knob
and ties my arms up
against the door. Williamsburg green.
With a touch as faint as a watermark.
Tracing cephalon, pygidium, glabella.

Swayback, through freshly cut stalks,
stalks the yellow cat. Can you smell
where analyses end, the orchard
oriole begins? Slap her breasts lightly
to see them quiver. Delighting in this.
Desiccation cracks and plant debris
throughout the interval. In the Black-
water River, fishnets float
from a tupelo's spongy root

chopped into corks. There may be sprawling
precursors, descendent clades there are none.

The gambit declined was less
promising. So the flock of crows
slaughtered all sixty lambs. Toward the east, red
and yellow colors prevail.
Praying at the graveside,
holding forth the palm of his hand
as a symbol of God's book.
For the entirety of the Ordovician.
With termites, Mrs. Elsinore explained,
as with the afterlife, remember:
there are two sides to the floor. A verb
for inserting and retrieving
green olives with the tongue. From
the scissure of your thighs.

In addition, the trilobites
were tectonically deformed. Snap-on
tools glinting from magenta
loosestrife, the air sultry
with creosote and cicadas.
You made me to lie down in a peri-Gondwanan back-arc basin.
Roses of wave ripples and gutter casts.
Your sex hidden by goat's beard.
Laminations in the sediment. All
preserved as internal molds
in a soft lilac shale.

Egrets picketing the spines of cattle in fields edged
with common tansy. Flowers my father gathered
for my mother to chew. To induce abortion. A common,
cosmopolitan agnostoid lithofacies naked in the foothills. I love
the character of your intelligence, its cast as well as pitch.
Border wide without marginal spines. At high angles
to the inferred shoreline.

It is the thin flute of the clavicles, each rain-pit
above them. The hypothesis of flexural loading. Aureoles
pink as steepleflower. One particular day, four hundred
million years ago, the mud stiffened
and held the stroke of waves. Orbital motion.
Raking leaves from the raspberries, you
uncover a nest of spring salamanders.

George Garrett

*Educated at Princeton, George Garrett is the current
poet laureate of Virginia. He has published eight
volumes of poetry from Louisiana State University
Press, including* The Reverend Ghost, Luck's
Shining Child, *and* Days of Our Lives Lie in
Fragments, *as well as several volumes of fiction.
Mr. Garrett has received fellowships from the
Guggenheim Foundation and the National
Endowment for the Arts and has won the Aiken-
Taylor Award for American Poetry, the T. S. Eliot
Award, and two prizes from the American Academy
of Arts and Letters.*

erf1

Figure of Speech

> It's a doggie dog world.
> —student paper

For years my litter of wounds
moved quietly, obedient and gentle,
well-trained, eager to please.
Loved my quick heels and the tight leash,
begged cutely, fetched and rolled over,
and licked the fingers that fed them.

Now they return, a gaunt and feral pack,
each and every one presenting
a noisy mouth, rich with cruel teeth
and drooling tongue. See their red eyes,
how the hair stands up as they turn against
each other, killing for my choicest parts.

The Long and the Short of It

(a letter to Brendan Galvin)

Over Peter Taylor's
brand new and expensive
toothpick fence,
through the glossy green
shine of my magnolia leaves,
directly into the back yard,
it could have been the ghost
of Ted Roethke or Big Jim
Dickey in a Halloween costume
or maybe even ole Galway Kinnell
cultivating his familiar image,
but was in fact a black
bear cub standing about six-four
and coming in at close to
three hundred pounds.
Quick and agile,
he was a real one like
one of yours, Brendan,
poet of the real and true,
his bristles stiff as a toilet brush
and a strong scent to raise hair
on the neck and back
of my black and tan hound
barking safely in the house.
Bear took one look at me
and the old cop and the young
Ranger with his tranquilizer gun,
then turned and went,
light as Baryshnikov,
over my ragged back hedge,
down the dry creek bed and,
quicker than I ever saw
anything larger than a squirrel
move, vanished into a shimmer

of leaves and afternoon light.
Forever as far as I was concerned.
Cop and Ranger lost him, too,
on the other side of Route 29
in a patch of pine woods near
the football practice field.
And that's about the size,
the long and short of it.
I don't know what it means,
Brendan, except that maybe
even an ordinary back yard
can yield up a share of
surprises. Meantime it gives
me plenty to think about.
I picture the bear, unnoticed,
joining in at football practice,
making the team, going to classes,
and on Saturday playing defense
against Virginia Tech,
first big game we won.
I picture a Tech player
complaining to his coach:
"Hey, coach, that guy
across from me, he's the ugliest
dude I've ever seen.
Got hair all over, head to toe,
red eyes and something like claws,
too; and I'm not going back
out there without a gun."

Main Currents of American Political Thought

(The Latest Version)

Founding Father (not King no never) George with all
those crude wooden teeth, not smiling often; Thomas Jefferson,

With giddy quill pen, gadgets, and a little mountain;
manic depressive Lincoln (and liberty too), to use an anachronistic

Goldwynism, all "blood and thirsty" and Jefferson
Davis in chains as later Nixon ought to have been, might have been
    too;

Teddy the Sisyphus of San Juan Hill (not Bunker)
and Franklin D., King of the Mountain, not charging up any hill,

Anywhere; LBJ holding court on the john and JFK,
bad back and all, back in the saddle again and again; and now

(Though Grant's the sad face on a fifty) a spoiled country boy
with bad temper and unquenchable appetites, "not tough but
    ruthless,"

Says a friend of this King of Hot Air; And I ask you:
was the man behind the curtain, any of the above, ever truly a wizard?

Margaret Gibson

Margaret Gibson has published six books of poetry,
including Icon and Evidence *(2001) and* Earth
Elegy: New and Selected Poems *(1997), both*
from Louisiana State University Press. Born in
Philadelphia in 1944 and educated at Hollins
College and the University of Virginia, Ms. Gibson
was a cowinner of the Melville Crane Award of the
Poetry Society of America for Out in the Open;
Memories of the Future: The Daybooks of Tina
Modotti. *Ms. Gibson is currently a visiting professor*
at the University of Connecticut.

Earthc Elegy

Rain on the shingles, on the maples—
this evening,
                    ground fog and cloud
mingled in the hollow between the ridges,
and a sorrow so gentle it could be

the mud I took this morning into my hands,
lifting it
                    from the garden's slump
of soil and rind, from its cursive sprawl
of blackened vine, turning the garden

after hard frost seared from purple
to black
                    the last cosmos.
I put down the shovel and took the damp
earth into my hands—

and when I broke the soft clay open
found
                    this twist of root

left out of last year's harvest, sown over
in spring, refired in the kiln of summer.

A hardened crust, nearly hollow. A blind
bounded thing,
                            so singular
nothing might divine it. *This is my body
broken*—once a sentence of breath

spun so vividly round I could put it
on my tongue,
                            and the words would
halo and hallow and blur my descent
into the barrow of unknowing

each moment is. No words now. Only this
root, humped
                            like a burial mound
and the hush of wondering what to pray,
knowing full well I have not loved,

I have not suffered, endangered, or enjoyed
enough of this world
                            to relinquish it
for another only made real by dying, or by
living in the holy world of words, apart

from what they point to. Here now, just
beyond the window glass,
                                        evening grosbeaks
gust and go. On the sill of the quiet rain
I put the root, and I sit with it,

into the night watching and waiting,
letting whatever words come
                            go off
on a spool of breath—until, silken
and sudden, from the pith

comes forth, nodding on its stem of dawn,
this day,
            unfolding itself
into the dark like a lily. And I sense
the quick of it, so tenderly nearing

it brushes aside its own icon screen
of bloom and root,
                black and gold—
and I am, crown to bole, just this sun
so recklessly arising.

Keeping Still

Because I saw
my mother, tense or careless, snap the string of her necklace,
a spill of beads shooting round on the floor,

I thought stars were so—
beads that could therefore be gathered, in one place cupped,
the sky held in a single crystal.

What is as patient, as still
as that thought? I am listening to the traffic into Boston,
how it swells and falls, in the rain a sea rushing

past the dark house.
I have followed as far as I can, leaning out of my skin, past the red
shift of car lights, through the tidal dark clouds to a misting of stars,

reaching, wanting more.
Even the galaxies, restless, are rolling farther, each from each,
on the face of eternity moving, a sweep of bright cells

rinsed daily away.
My heart is not quiet. I want the faith that moves mountains.
I want the bright force that holds them still.

How can anyone stunned by the night's consolation of stars
dare say, *I have not seen what I want*—
and yet, I say it.

Presque Isle

Stone markers, ashes, the self—
I know we must consider these. But the lake
               is as mortal. And that is
why the earth seems to rest in silent meditation,
      the leaves of the sun
              blowing gold and claret and sherry—
this white sand ridge, solid enough to walk on,
      moving in truth like a cloud.
          If I could muster it, I'd be
an unknowing as winged, as seamless as these
      flashes of scarlet
              intermittence you say are
woodpeckers, having constructed each one
      from the hollow rattle of its call
              and the pattern of black and white
and brilliant red that drills on the broken baroque
      of these old oaks.
              Headstrong, momentary,
they are what I cannot see looking. But just look
      into those bald, black
              imperturbable eyes—
unblinking passionless. There's the unknowable, that's
      what does as it must,
              without thinking it,
seeing everything as it is, unlike nothing else,
      and God.

Nikki Giovanni

Nikki Giovanni was born in Knoxville in 1943 and holds the University Distinguished Professor chair at Virginia Tech. She is a member of the national advisory board of the Underground Railroad Freedom Center and a recipient of both the Virginia Governor's Award and the 1996 Langston Hughes Award. Her most recent books include Blues: For All the Changes *(1999),* The Selected Poems of Nikki Giovanni *(1997), and* The Love Poems of Nikki Giovanni *(1996), all published by William Morrow.*

Knoxville, Tennessee

I always like summer
best
you can eat fresh corn
from daddy's garden
and okra
and greens
and cabbage
and lots of
barbecue
and buttermilk
and homemade ice-cream
at the church picnic
and listen to
gospel music
outside
at the church
homecoming
and go to the mountains with
your grandmother
and go barefooted

and be warm
all the time
not only when you go to bed
and sleep

Nikki-Rosa

childhood remembrances are always a drag
if you're Black
you always remember things like living in Woodlawn
with no inside toilet
and if you become famous or something
they never talk about how happy you were to have
your mother
all to yourself and
how good the water felt when you got your bath
from one of those
big tubs that folk in chicago barbecue in
and somehow when you talk about home
it never gets across how much you
understood their feelings
as the whole family attended meetings about Hollydale
and even though you remember
your biographers never understand
your father's pain as he sells his stock
and another dream goes
And though you're poor, it isn't poverty that
concerns you
and though they fought a lot
it isn't your father's drinking that makes any difference
but only that everybody is together and you
and your sisters have happy birthdays and very good
Christmasses
and I really hope no white person ever has cause
to write about me
because they never understand

Black love is Black wealth and they'll
probably talk about my hard childhood
and never understand that
all the while I was quite happy

51

Fred C. Tom

John Haines

*Born in Norfolk, Virginia, in 1924 and currently a
resident of Montana, John Haines began writing
poetry in Alaska in 1947. He served in the Navy
in World War II and has taught at the University
of Montana, the University of Washington, and the
University of Alaska. He published* For the Century's
End *(University of Washington) in 2001 and* The
Owl in the Mask of the Dreamer *(Graywolf)
in 1996.*

The Stone Harp

A road deepening in the north,
strung with steel,
resonant in the winter evening,
as though the earth were a harp
soon to be struck.

As if a spade
rang in a rock chamber:

in the subterranean light,
glittering with mica,
a figure like a tree turning to stone
stands on its charred roots
and tries to sing.

Now there is all this blood
flowing into the west,
ragged holes at the waterline of the sun—
that ship is sinking.

And the only poet is the wind,
a drifter
who walked in from the coast
with empty pockets.

He stands on the road
at evening, making a sound
like a stone harp
strummed
by a handful of leaves . . .

The Weaver

for Blair

By a window in the west
where the orange light falls,
a girl sits weaving in silence.

She picks up threads of sunlight,
thin strands from the blind shadows
fallen to the floor,
as her slim hands swiftly pass
through cords of her loom.

Light from a wine glass
goes into the weave,
light passing from the faces
of those who watch her;
now the grey flash from a mirror
darkening against the wall.

And her batten comes down,
softly beating the threads,
a sound that goes and comes again,
weaving this house and the dusk
into one seamless, deepening cloth.

Brand

I have followed you as far as I can,
darkness falls in the wood.

I touch your tree, I cannot reach you:
dry burrs and scales,
bark that scrapes my hands.

What will you do if I leave?
Grow dense and hard, sinking forever
inside the wood that holds you,
your face an effigy under the vines.

I feel myself stiffen like you,
an old mistrust driven like a thorn
into the tree of my flesh.

I will close this part of the forest,
bar the road with a thicket—
ivy or rhododendron,
something I know you loved.
No one will come, and no bird sing
from these shuttered boughs.

I leave with a living branch
seized from the wrack between us:
brand or torch,
green knot of desire
by which I will see my way.

Dan Smith

Cathryn Hankla

Cathryn Hankla was born in Richlands, Virginia, in 1958 and graduated from Hollins College, where she is now a professor of English. She serves as poetry editor of the Hollins Critic. *Her collections of poetry from Louisiana State University Press include* Poems for the Pardoned *(2002),* Texas Schoolbook Depository *(2000),* Negative History *(1997), and* Afterimages *(1991). Her novel,* A Blue Moon in Pale Water, *was recently reissued as a paperback by the University of Virginia Press.*

Encounter

Out of dusky silence and staggering
Time, from a swollen afternoon
Of elevated leg and pain killers,

Comes the car and driver. If thoughts
Briefly divert, their range is narrow:
Bucks in rut routinely damage vehicles

Along this stretch. The shoulders
Are carefully scanned. Her father
Wrecked last week and may not recover.

The driver, doubly chastened, still doesn't see
A black angus leveraging for broke,
Head bowed to barbed wire, munching

With backside and all fours planted
In the road. It's over almost before
It begins: red car bounces into oncoming lane,

Radiator leaks fluorescent green,
Black angus veers off its hooves, releasing
Anguished groans. Its orange-tagged ear

Writhes and slumps. The driver stumbles
From her car into the shadowed weeds,
Alone. Wind chills her to the bone.

On Athena's Shoulder

The owl's cat eyes echoed the highbeams
and I swerved. I knew nothing more.
It had lighted on the country road
some time before. I took the last curve

and dipped down a slope
where I had once spun on ice,
end over beginning, like a planet
toppled in the tilt of seasons.

Hearing, still, the voices of the evening
and my own erratic wisdom
looping in my inner ear, I almost missed
the horned owl swiveling to confront me

with its white throat. All of the words
in my head turned, then, into owls.
At the center of every question hunched
a silent owl, a silent way of knowing.

And I was left wondering
whether field mouse or broken wing
had downed it there, wondering who
would come along and hit it square.

Henry Hart

Henry Hart, a humanities professor at the College of William and Mary, is the author of two books of poems, The Rooster Mask *(University of Illinois 1998) and* The Ghost Ship *(North Starline 1990). Born in 1954 in Connecticut, Mr. Hart is also the author of critical studies on Robert Lowell, Geoffrey Hill, and Seamus Heaney, as well as a biography,* James Dickey: The World as Lie *(Picador 2000). He is a former editor of* Verse *and received a National Endowment for the Arts fellowship in 1998.*

Pocahontas in Jamestown

It was the wrong day to canoe along the James.
Brittle shells of ice still clung to banks.
Clouds puffed from the power plant, radiant and deformed.

I wanted to get close enough to hear the stories
children pressed from metal boxes on the walks,
but the river scrambled words in breaking waves.

Aren't origins all the same? One tribe
killing another, then lying about the dead?
Statues never admit what lies in graves.

Pocahontas wears buckskin fringe she never wore.
Her bronze skin grows greener every year.
Pollen dusts her feathered hair to gold.

What did she think when she saw those first
shallops bob like black-backed gulls toward shore,
bearded faces muttering oaths at common shrubs?

Did she think, "Let's beat them back to sea
with thorn-tipped clubs"? Or did she lug
baskets of maize and squash to where they knelt?

Her tongue still sticks in bronze. Final answers
decay in unmarked graves around her feet.
Her story lies with bones in an English plot.

Imagine her in London. Fog and coal soot
curdling over sewers near the Belle Sauvage.
White ruff tightening around her neck like rope.

She died at Gravesend before her ship sailed home.
The eroding James sank Jamestown's fort in silt.
Fire sailed ash from roofs across the waves.

How do tourists read those voices children tease
from boxes on the walks? How do they glean
what happened from a tour guide's talk?

Her eyes point old questions at the sun.
Tarnished hands catch what answers light can give.
Wind numbs our ears with static, and we paddle home.

Notes from Mount Vernon

If I could carry the olive twig
like the weathervane dove
and offer it to lightning
or pluck from wind its seeds

of hail knocking gables;
if I could scry in crystals
of snow a map
of unarguable directives,

and watch the future drip
from the cupola's icicles—
I would hammer my skin
into bronze feathers

and stand forever
in the ridgepole's weather.
But the century winds
in ice towards zero.

I wanted to be the hero
of enlightenment!
Marrying farmer and financier,
cotton field and iron forge!

But ended in this grave of symbols,
referee for Jefferson
pitching his eclogues
at Hamilton's redcoats.

Why did I ride the white horse
into battle? For yokels
who hated the army
more than King George's taxes?

Though they stamped me
on a dollar, I was the watermark
on my will, guiding
a plow with a flower,

the bronze dove
with an olive twig,
shedding rain
across the divided furrows.

David Huddle

*David Huddle was born in 1942 in Ivanhoe, Virginia,
served in Vietnam, and received his education at
the University of Virginia, Hollins College, and
Columbia University. He has taught literature and
writing at the University of Vermont since 1971 and
is also a faculty member at the Bread Loaf School
of English. The author of five collections of short
stories, a book of essays, and a novel, Mr. Huddle
has published four volumes of poetry, most recently*
Summer Lake: New and Selected Poems
(Louisiana State University 1999).

Threshing Wheat

My job was to hold the bags
at the end of the chute,
grain sometimes coming down
fast and thick as water.
I grunted to lift those bags,
and Crow Jim'd spit and cuss
me out if I slipped and let
any wheat spill on the ground.
I liked to chew that stuff,
making something somewhere between
chewing gum and bread in my mouth.
One day up in Jim Early's field,
we saw a buck deer, antlers big
as rocking chairs, being chased
by dogs, come out of the woods,
stand still there a minute looking
at the trucks, the tractor, that
house-sized threshing machine,
the men with pitchforks and one
boy scuttering all around.
Then slow as in a dream it
jumped the fence and loped easy

down the hill, the dogs still
yapping back up in the woods.
We all stopped work and hollered
until Peaks told us to get off
our asses and start earning our pay.
In the back of the pickup going
home, we talked about that deer:
Crow Jim swore if he'd had a gun
he'd have shot it, Hitler saying
he'd seen plenty bigger, and Monkey
patting that New Testament he kept
in his top overalls pocket, pulling
me over so close beside him I could
smell the sweat and whispering it
was a sign sent down by God.

Study

This morning rain on my skylight
marbles the blue-gray sky and blurs
the maple's branches suffering
the wind from the northeast.
                                    A bird
flashes diagonally up
across the wet-streaked glass,
winged shadow there and gone so fast
I barely see it;
                        then standing
at my grandmother's grave, I feel
my mother lean against me, wind
and cold rain slapping our faces
for letting Gran die by herself
in a hateful room;
                        and driving
through mountains in a slick-tired VW
with one headlight gone, I'm swabbing

fog off the windshield while rain turns
to snow;
            dark is coming, and I
am saying good-bye to Linda
Butler on Dundalk Avenue
in thin rain that's chilling us both,
shivering us hard these minutes
that are the last we ever spend
together;
            a boy on a porch
smells rain coming across the fields
and sees his young father running
toward him with drops splattering
his shirt;
            a child out in the yard
hears his aunt laugh as he strips off
clothes in a thunderstorm—
                    quick light
flashing down corridors darkened
by all these years!—
                as a crow lights,
bobbing a limb of my neighbor's spruce,
or lifts and flies through fifty miles
of rain before it comes to rest.

Model Father

Now when I say my father
—meaning his smell of carbide
and cigarettes, his curtain
of opened and held-up
newspaper, the red dents
at either side of the bridge
of his nose, the parchment skin
on the backs of his hands,
and his thick thumb that to me
meant he was a grown man

and that has in recent years
attached itself to my hand—

I'm really saying my father isn't
in my life anymore, except
in just this way—when I choose
words to assemble him,
as when he and I sometimes chose
to spend a Saturday afternoon
at a newspaper-covered card table
gluing together small pieces
of balsa, keeping quiet
company without much regard
for whether or not what
we made would fly.

T. R. Hummer

T. R. Hummer, current editor of the Georgia
Review, *has also edited the* Kenyon Review *and*
New England Review. *A Mississippi native born
in 1950, he is the author of many books of poems,
including* The Angelic Orders, The Passion of
the Right-Angled Man, Lower-Class Heresy,
Walt Whitman in Hell, *and* Useless Virtues.
*He has received fellowships from the National
Endowment for the Arts and the Guggenheim
Foundation, and he recently taught at Virginia
Commonwealth University.*

Heresies, Overheard

At the corner church, colored light cantilevers harsh
Against this winter night through the body of Christ crucified
In stained glass. The heavy-handed
                              lead lines that define
His suffering shape show black in the relief of absolute contrast.
He fluoresces above the invitation of an open double door
Where some carpenter framed him up
                              as the architect planned, exact
And clichéd in translucent mimesis of flesh. Inside
It's prayer meeting night and they sing all together,
Maybe a hundred voices
                    skewed in their Protestant unison.
You want to talk theory, you want to talk the beautiful
And dangerous discipline of strictured harmony?
You've come to the wrong place, brother.
                              Here they all believe
In the singular voice, here they make one note
Stand for everything. Where I am it's night,
And the myths say dark brings evil,
                              but this time it only brings me,
Strolling the root-heaved sidewalk, happy and going nowhere.

It brings a great cold sky full of the unflinching light
Of winter stars, which are not arranged
                                        in lopsided dot-to-dot
Cave wall drawings of animals or gods. As far as I can see,
Which straight up is pretty far, they tell no stories.
Tonight all the beautiful and dangerous
                                        stories are gone,
All passed from me: the one about the woman, about the boy I was,
About me, mother, father. It's cold, and my breath is a Christ-colored
    cloud
Of human steam where I stand
                                        in my brilliant angle of churchlight.
That fact, now, is all I am. Above me, the stigmata
Are perfect circles of clear bloodred. Sweet Jesus died
At the hands of storytellers.
                                        There was one who told us
Christ never suffered, his body was unreal. That was a heresy,
The critics said. They gave it a name and a dark denouement.
Every body's a critic, even the preacher's,
                                        which quavers its off-
Key tenor against the perfect pitch of electric organ. The song
    he sings
Elucidates his text. And it's true: to have no flesh
Is to have no voice in the matter.
                                        That's why I stand
Silent here between starlight and glasslight. The stories
Are lifted, vanished, even the one I like to call my life.
They'll be back, but for now I'm plotless,
                                        and even the body fades
To dark as I walk on, happy, self-forgotten, whistling a random tune
Nameless and unrepeatable, but whose rhythm is the wrenched
    and real
Shape of the sidewalk and the way I stumble on
                                        my own amazing grace.

Zeitgeist Lightning

What were the doctors doing with old Whitman's brain
When it slipped through their fingers? *Anthropometry,*
The biographies tell us: *the measure of* quote
Man unquote —
                    weighing and assessing that most god-
Like tumor of consciousness; mapping out the seat
Of the archangel whose occult name is Genius.
A laboratory worker accidentally
Dropped it on the floor.
                    Had he put it in a jar?
He was an intern from Des Moines, say, whose mother
Had pawned, well, anything you care to imagine.
Where was his mind? He sat up late the night before
Rereading *Song of Myself.*
                    He knew what he was
Up against. And then the lapse, the hideous mess
On the clinical tile. Will he ever forget
The pure mortification of it? Years pass. Conrad
Writes *Lord Jim,* America elects
                    Coolidge, Hoover,
Karloff makes *Frankenstein,* in which the doctor's mad
Assistant drops the normal brain and substitutes
A murderer's — and still that humiliation
Goes through him every time
                    he closes his eyes. *Fool,*
The body's own voices accuse: *incompetent.*
He was exhausted, worried, overworked, in debt,
Depressed. All beside the point. His shame defines him.
In the Iowa sky
                lightning leaps its mystic
Synapse. Somewhere a war is starting. Nurses stand
At the bedside holding hypodermics, glucose.
Idiot, destroyer! So this is death at last,
Not at all what he expected —
                    more disgusting,

More demeaning. Trucks swarm the highway west of town.
Everything is flattened. Now the doctor tightens
The immaculate bolt in his neck, as the brain—
Whose?—throbs in its bloody rhythm.

                                      Yet he can love
Himself completely, even stitched together as
He is. And the rest of us? Where has consciousness
Struck? No matter how we long to drop it, we will
Not crack the convoluted
                        matter of its lines.

Friendly Fire

> Land war will require the most complex
> combat flying ever flown, with more
> tragedies of friendly fire inevitable.
> —CNN newscast, 2/4/91

Heraclitean, for instance: the world as a gaseous
Shimmer, like afterburner fumes in the oily night sky
Outside Carbondale, where lovers pass through the flux
Of the heart's napalm— or alchemical: the transformative image
Of the sun over Dallas, antiseptic if you could touch it,
Tritely aetherial, the volatile gold of gas-well burn-off
On the freeway's horizon, cauterizing, uncorrupting bone—
We could imagine anything. Suppose we pulled a lever
And every carburetor in Charlottesville
Detonated in a transcendental rush of vesicatory gas
And oxyacetylene? What would we think we were seeing?
What residue would remain?
                              I think it would be elemental.
I think it would be pure. I think it would give off the smell
Of brass, chrysanthemums, caustic old velour—
Or that strange metallic odor that drags my grandmother's face
Up from the flare of my neurons, where the innocent dead all go:
A bombed-out country no body belongs to, untouchable, chemical,
   clean.

Julia Johnson

*Born in New Orleans in 1971, Julia Johnson lives in
Roanoke and is currently an assistant professor
of English at Hollins University. Her first book is*
Naming the Afternoon (*Louisiana State University
2002*). *Ms. Johnson's poems have appeared in* 64,
New Orleans Review, *and* Poetry International.

October in Virginia

It is with ease that we break free,
ride our saddles thin as ice, we spin
in the moment's red glaze, an avenue wide
and green. You know what blames this truth,
sideways like a deer's clear vision.
The rain has stopped, the length
of a minute lengthens like a thin strand of yarn
from a blanket. It is cold as ever.
The robins have little to do but shiver.
The windows of the room have all but disappeared.
Branches break, bones on the face caught,
cupped, canned in what seems an hour.
Her body loosens and the wind, gray and odd,
wraps around this small house.

In the morning, bleached sky over an unmoving
pond, a puddle in the brain. The cat leaps
from a steel tube and lands, solid and still.
Underneath it all, the ground must leak a slow leak.

The Drive

It's time the fireflies live long,
leap into the field's palm,
a cold clasp on the locket of the lip

like the highway's strip of light never ending,
slim and blurred across the view, I too
become a kind of edge, the bitten hold.

It's time the ducks waste their white wings,
move along in the lagoon, brave
and without what once held them to be white.

It's time there is light on this wide expanse,
the face's frequent expression, telling
the hand's off-hand remark, surfacing,
the wheel catching what sound now held there.

It's time this dark space separates what true inches
there are, odd, even, or split, shoulder to shoulder,
edge to edge, the creek rises, a black line outside the window.

Sam Kashner

Sam Kashner, born in 1954 and currently a resident of Williamsburg, Virginia, is the author of three books of poetry: Driving at Night, No More Mr. Nice Guy, *and* Don Quixote in America. *He has coauthored two works of nonfiction with Nancy Schoenberger. Mr. Kashner works as a freelance writer for* Vanity Fair *and* GQ.

Vehemence & Opinions

Oh empty heart,
virile as five sailors!
Accidents fertilize the rocks
that cry out
"what is left for me?"
while smoke rises from the outhouse,
or is it steam from a broken shell?
The rain stops us from growing.
A lifting of the covers
reveals a cannibal
who once marched in a procession.
Dark as an orchard they moved
toward the city hall,
their baskets swaying in the wind.
It was a storm full of mushrooms
that cannot be eaten.
We choose to leave our
garbage in the snow,
held back by a wreath of bricks,
sunlight twitching on the ground
like someone stepping into a puddle.
Life shifts and passes
with a curtain's shudder,
the heart a painted clock.

Unidentifiable in Rain

What did I do wrong?
The autumn cherry, untied,
hidden behind the shed,
comes upon us like a thought,
determinate and tender.

The spokes of a wheel
go around our breathing.
The city air has a siren in it.
The children wake up
confused as ghosts
trampled in their clothes.

A sad nerve runs through the streets
where blueberries reflect the absent night,
which is never as feminine as air
or the giggling perspective
of what passes bitterly between travelers.
Winter fills our mood
like jars made of earth
that the earth abandons.

What matters in our village
is the threnody of moccasins and ink.
The stars groan with their unfortunate
dinginess, hanging out for everyone to see.
We discover our opposites in these postures
that cake over and break our will.

The birds hum without questions
in the air of silk, and after them
the clouds appear above the gum trees—
which is where onyx is made.

And you have won the prize
delivered out of love.   We have
saved it for you like an ending, the one
that comes along once in a lifetime.
Your profile is the face of god
who beckons us into this garden
overgrown with tears.

Sally Keith

Sally Keith was born in Charlottesville in 1973 and grew up in Fairfax, Virginia. She was educated at Bucknell University, George Mason University, and the University of Iowa and now teaches at Rhode Island College. Her poems have appeared in Field, Quarterly West, *and* Ohio Review. *Her first book,* Design *(Center for Literary Publishing 2000), received the Colorado Prize for Poetry.*

The Hunters

Their return didn't flutter, what body it had
     tamped — moved in slow progression
their legs leaving hollowed dents

     in snow; the dogs, behind them, hanging
their heads, then, further — something between
     desperation and attempt. Here,

the knot on the nerve in my neck, *mark me* —
     my armor incomplete;
the dark color shuffling, thicker

     than cards and thicker than rope, and
the quicker the speed the harder
     my hope — The hunters (call them: knights, call

their armor: burlap sacks, call their swords: wooden
     shafts) have almost cleared the wood. Count
the few bare elms. They dodge them, according to

     gravitational chance. The rods go down
with the slant of the hill and the hurry of dogs
     sounds on their heels — they keep it at their backs.

Walk in these woods. Leave that. I'd pull down
        my woolen cap, cinch my tired eyes
to my feet. What can they wear, that would let me—

        when I am handed over? What will I speak?
Can the village know? Couched in hills it holds
        a solemn hum against the thicker,

blacker beat. And the cottages line the rectangular
        lake. And the lake is frozen. And the children,
unaware of their pattern, gleefully skate. The wind

        is the only resistance they know. *Mark me.*
Death is the pebble, is slipped from the bridge
        as we finish descending the hill, slipped

by the unknown foot. Listen. It hits. *Leave*
        that. Listen. The children are shrieking.
Shall not. Shall not. Pull down my woolen cap.

        Now, Sunday morning, we return. No
children. The steeple, inextricable—the given
        in a village shape. We look to it. Tomorrow and—

Mercy. Mercy. Death is—
        The ghost. The choir. The almost sound
rising up. Belt, breastplate, helmet, my sword

        of—this skin beats too fast. *Walk in*
these woods. There were three birds, wing touching
        contented. I am returning, I'll sit

by the fire with my only wife. I'll go
        for bread by dawn and wood by dusk.
I'll study the bird that is left, cutting

        winter's only sky. Lonely,
or, at last. *Mercy. Mark me.* To hold it—
        feathered and nothing. I'd try.

Rod Smith

Sarah Kennedy

Sarah Kennedy teaches literature and writing at
Mary Baldwin College. Born in Indiana in 1960,
she holds a Ph.D. in Renaissance poetry from Purdue
University and an M.F.A. in poetry from Vermont
College. She is the author of three books of poetry,
Double Exposure *(Cleveland State University*
2003), Flow Blue *(Elixir Press Prize 2002), and*
From the Midland Plain *(Tryon 1999). In 2001,*
she received both the Nebraska Review *and* Flyway
awards in poetry.

Flow Blue

In the antique store, a chipped tea set:
cobalt vines and flowers pressed into white
porcelain. Lifting the one uncracked plate,
I see two women turn their backs. My husband
once dated the dark one, who leans
toward her companion, *Every few years,*
he finds his god again between the legs
of some dumb teenager. My cheeks burn,
and staring down, I remember my friend Kim
sketching, with a ball point, a snaky Satan
twisting his tongue up the leg of a naked Eve,
her face pansy-soft, just before Sister Mary Catherine
sneaked up behind us and boxed her ears.
Someone taps my shoulder and I almost drop
the dish. The shop owner asks if I like
what I've chosen. I don't know what it is,
and he laughs. *What would a young girl like you*
know about old things? It's flow blue:
color has bled through the china's white skin.
If this were red, I'd describe it as a blush,
he says, tracing a finger along the pattern.
I buy it for a table by the window
in my living room. Through the pane,

I can see swirling lines and blossoms,
a penetrating indigo, and standing
out here, I'd say it looks like a bruise.

Ewe

She must have been heavy with wool
by late winter, and I might have plunged
my hands, wrist-deep, into her plush,
the soft strands sweetly greasing my fingers.
Surely, she heaved, helpless, for hours,

and I probably raised my unsteady self
to cry out to my absent husband,
to the empty field, *Where the hell are you?*
Then she lay too quiet in the crisp,
tawny grass, and I either wept

or sweated my face damp, but at last
I cleared my eyes, thrust one hand deep
inside her, found the small hooves, pointed
backward, and pulled. The lamb
resisted, stretched, then slipped, still

in its sac, onto my lap. I rubbed,
pounded, and wasn't I astonished
by the joy of seeing that new-drawn body
stand, punch its mother's teats and drink?
It must have been so, but

I remember her blood and birth-fluid
veining my arm to the elbow. I know
I could not look away from my skin,
glistening with the oily traces of all
the other ways this might have ended.

Sin

The broomstick struck soft skin
and my breath caught with pleasure,
but my sister's cry startled me to tear
the pillowcase from my eyes. Doubled

over, she clutched her face. I'd thrust
hard instead of swinging a gentle arc
around the basement—a version
of blindman's buff forbidden by our father,

sure we'd break a bone or the ceiling lights.
But sick of pokes in my back, I'd jabbed
at her laughter. Smaller, I didn't expect
to win, and I knew what was coming

when she rose, angry eye already swollen
and bloodshot. Dad saved me that time,
bellowing our names, and, sudden allies yelling
Molly fell, we tore upstairs. Old news

to our parents by dinner, the red dot
in my sister's gaze fell on me all evening.
For days, I stayed in our father's sight,
prayed as I should, but the bruise refused

to fade until I swept her room immaculate,
even beyond the clean of Dad's white glove.
I plotted my next move while she pointed to specks,
elbowing me to show where I'd missed a spot.

Thomas LeCro

Peter Klappert

*Peter Klappert lives in Alexandria and teaches in
the graduate writing program at George Mason
University. He was born in 1942 and grew up in
Rowayton, Connecticut. His* Lugging Vegetables to
Nantucket *received the Yale Younger Poets Prize in
1971; his other collections include* Chokecherries:
New and Selected Poems 1966−1999 *(Orchises
2000) and* The Idiot Princess of the Last Dynasty
(Knopf 1984).

Bright Moments Lakeside

A derelict, half-hidden boat house,
rusty pump house, and a long flat causeway dam
rampant with summer grasses. Cowpads,
a few crows lifting off them as you walk.

Bright moments lakeside: flickers, wrens,
chicka-dee-dee-dees (they like to hang out
with titmice). A bullfrog—two frogs—leap
from the duckweed (I don't see any ducks).

Color coming awake—yellow, orchid,
magenta—in cinquefoil, smartweed, false
strawberry, dianthus or Deptford pink,
alfalfa or cow vetch (such confusion
in the common names!). Two or three
kinds of clover, two or three kinds of bees.
A cedar and scruffy shrubs crowd
the low barbed wire fence along the dam.
Back toward the boat house, pickerel weed
rising up out of the shallows

floats its purple-blue flowers on emerald clouds.
No one much sees this, I guess. Only
the locals who come in pick-ups

across the fields at evening, who climb
up here with cigarettes, chips and six-packs

to wait for bass and bream. And the cows.
The hull says *Arkansas Traveler.* Dented
and camouflage peeling and two seats broken,
an old aluminum boat nuzzles the dam.
A dark green board and a coffee can
soak in the bilge, dragonflies ride the gunwales.
Oar locks, but no oars.
                              A jump-rope painter.

Chokecherries

Thirty feet from my windows,
an old kennel-wire fence
thickly grown over with honeysuckle,
poison ivy, and wild roses
just beginning to open
into the loose sort of droopy garlands
an aesthetic young farmer
might drape around Elsie
or Dobbin.

          Where the wire ends
and the knotted up, spiraling vines
paw toward more light, six slim
grey trunks of chokecherry
feather into leaves and
clusters or blossoming fronds
that lift and fall with the breeze
like diminutive mare's tails
—each separate flower a rose,
each separate flower
three-eighths of an inch of
white disk, radiant
about a head of yellow-gold stamens.

Beyond the chokecherries
and a rutted road, beyond
locust posts and barbed wire,
a deepening pasture lights up
with *ranunculus*, "little frogs"
for some reason, lights up
—in fact—with buttercups
as clouds move sunlight around.

And beyond them, veiled
and perhaps faintly blue
in the distance, broadly
lit by the same shifting light,
four rounded green mountains,
on the nearest and tallest of which
someone has built a white silo
and low barn—or more likely
some kind of radar station
that talks all night to darkness,
some kind of early warning,
perhaps an observatory.

                                I'm
just happy to stand here
and hold my vote close,
white-blinded and stupidly
gazing into random galaxies
and minor constellations, starbursts
of yellow-haired stamens
in white corollas.

T. H. Mesner

Jeanne Larsen

*Born in Washington, D.C., in 1950, Jeanne Larsen
grew up on army posts in Virginia, Kansas, Pennsylva-
nia, and West Germany. She is the author of* James
Cook: In Search of Terra Incognita *(University of
Virginia 1980), as well as* Manchu Palaces *(1996),*
Bronze Mirror *(1991), and* Silk Road *(1989), all
from Henry Holt. Among Ms. Larsen's many awards
are a Japan/U.S. Friendship Commission Award in
creative nonfiction, a National Endowment for the
Arts grant for poetry translation, and two poetry prizes
from the Academy of American Poets. Ms. Larsen
received her education at Oberlin College, Hollins
College, and the University of Iowa, and she is
currently a professor of English at Hollins.*

Turning the Edge

Go out in the morning.
Cross to the next,
the great, valley, squinting
in the unexpected
crosslight. Both ridges
have been lumbered, plowed,
planted with houses or
let run to second growth.
Go, cut saplings,
build a raft, float it
down the James. Drown
your ax, the blade's marred.
Approaching the gorge
(it is afternoon now)
you cross corrugated shadows
of young trees.
                    The rapids: now
hold to the pressure,
the turning edge.

After the Rains

After the rains,
clearing. Our first sight:
the moon hooks its tail

as if nothing had changed.
Four weeks of rain
come to an end. How many times

have I wakened beside you?
I remember I smashed
all my mirrors, cut moorings,

moved in. I forget all the rest.
What's left to us?
Silt clogs the spillways,

the dam roars, young willows
choke on the floodplain.
We fling on our coats,

rush, wordless; the lake
presses and presses the flank of the marsh.
Mists rise from new pools,

slip their arms round our waists,
murmur promises, plead with us,
stroke our faces, coax smiles.

Under the spruces, we lose the moon.
The trail turns. You vanish, ahead.
Deep in the woods, I look back and see

a long unknown figure
speeding white, flickering
in dim light past thin trunks.

Edward C. Lynskey

*Born in Arlington in 1956, Edward C. Lynskey
received both his B.A. and M.A. from George Mason
University. A self-employed software engineer, he has
published three books of poetry,* The Tree Surgeon's
Gift *(Scripta Humanistica 1990),* Teeth of the
Hydra *(Crop Dust 1986), and* Wrought Iron
*(Northern Virginia Community College 1980). His
work has also appeared in the* Atlantic Monthly,
Plainsongs, *and* American Poetry Review.

In Search of Our Father's Guitar and Gin

You do love sloe gin. You want the burn
of it on your liver like a steeple
on fire, a straw child charring to golliwog.
"Darker the devil's lyric, the harsher
the gin," you'd slur, Gibson a full fig
eight strung on knee, a dancehall doxy.
Your scarred, creosote fingers fretted

offkey to Tubb's Texas waltz, to Husky's
thrush wings but you never got to pick.
And every crimson wink by the cautionary
light aslant the radio tower, a flypaper
angel struck you with a brown bottle flu:
death of glassy eyed, low-luck lurchers.
Then bells hanging in the church inferno

crashed, heavy with grief, grave clappers
hushed, a wreck painted demolition red.
Gin Glands, Hell's at hand, the deuce sits
sawing a maple fiddle, one hundred proof.
And you'll kiss through the smoke your
Harshener, nary a drip or drop of dry gin,
and father, eternity is a slow, sad chug.

Persephone in West Virginia

At April's surge, this odd girl
tiptoed out of a disused coal
shaft, her shawl a foreign blue

used to polish satellite dishes,
tv signals beaming in gin-clear.
She settled in an RV, cultivated

cannas inside old white-walled
slicks off a dirt-track Camaro,
carved cherry logs with a Stihl

chainsaw into newts and trolls
schoolkids took home. Summer
soon gone, a huge harvest moon

bowled over chopped cornfields
big-bellied doves banqueted in.
Migrant apple-pickers scuttled

away trailorloads; cider presses
oozed overtime. Along Blue Suck
Falls they became that fortunate

few to view her airborne mystery,
singing to pry open a frosty maw,
singing to go under before winter.

Heather Ross Miller

*Heather Ross Miller was born in Albemarle, North
Carolina, in 1939 and was educated at the
University of North Carolina — Greensboro. The
recipient of two fellowships from the National
Endowment for the Arts, Ms. Miller has been Thomas
H. Broadus Professor of English at Washington and
Lee University for the past decade. Her collections of
poetry include* Friends and Assassins *(1993) and*
Hard Evidence *(1990), both from the University
of Missouri Press, and* Horse Horse Tyger Tyger
*(1973) from Red Clay Press. Her most recent books are
a novel and a memoir.*

Cloudless Sulfur, Swallowtail, Great Spangled Fritillary

Out of willows and milkweed and woods around water,
tight tangled places, came her husband's body count.
His atrocities spotted as dice, perfect specimens,
black pansy faces, purple and cream, plain sulfur,
checkerboard, some females
with powdery fringes and starred wings,
they lay under glass in her husband's room,
where she never went if she could help,
except to pull down windows in a rain.
Brutalities pleased him,
these antennae feeble as her own eyelash,
his willful treasures, his dried perfection.
She breathed on the butterflies,
and her breath flexed, then shriveled,
pungent as blue Windex
she sprayed on his mirror. Later,
she slept in the den, forgetting him,
fortunes and blood spattering the TV screen.
Spring Azures tormented her dreams, the tangled array
of Swallowtails, zebra and tiger, black white,
white yellow, blue black blue, pieces

of purple Mourning Cloaks.
Barbarous screams.
His screams.

She woke, face pressed like a waffle, blinking,
her breath no breath, caught in a net, the stinging
unrelenting ether filling up all the space
beyond the moon, between the stars, the upper
upper regions, volatile, colorless, and highly
flammable. A terrible struggle for air.

Good Colds

Letting loose fragrances of camphor,
eucalyptus, menthol, the burning oil of clove,
my grandmother jabbed Vicks
down her throat and never gagged.
I longed for the shape she made
against her linen shade, a big
blue-shadowed warmth, nest-builder,
while birds in the chimney
flexed their dark wings, taunting
Does this mean anything?
I thought I might drown,
sitting big-eyed on her bed
like the asthmaed Buddha,
the flannel congested Jesus.
In the end she layered my lungs
with the same slime, unselfish
and useful, weathered me for whatever
and where, anointed and spiced me
for who and for what breathing,
it does not matter. The dark wings
in the chimney clothed my mind,
the soot fell like snow, and we both
breathed off to bed.

If you hear of such a healer,
if any such healer hears me,
I need to know.

Sleepwalker

My mirror is a forty-year-old moon.
The moon is a small bland Nazarene,
her hair parted down the middle,
sleeping. Out in the kitchen
the Hoot's Hardware calendar scythes off
my breath in phases full new old wasted.
Here I circle a day, total a week.
I start to wake up and tell you people something,
but my face in the moon blurs.
What I want to tell you is I still like to look pretty
but the Nazarene won't. I still like to wake up,
sure, even before I lift and shift her eyes,
sure my face is a mild familiar prize
Hoot's Hardware gives to fishermen.
Throw your hook here in these waters.
Smallmouth strike easy, I'd tell them.
Trout sip white flies from the surface
and catfish come to the hand. Look,
I'm your pinup sweetheart!

But the bland Nazarene parts my hair
straight down the middle, sighs
"Shut up" in my face,
and the mean calendar sharpens its scythes.

Elizabeth Seydel Morgan

*Elizabeth Seydel Morgan was born in Atlanta in
1939. She graduated from Hollins College and now
lives in Richmond and Amherst County. She has been
a visiting faculty member at Washington and Lee
University and Randolph-Macon Woman's College
and is the author of three collections from Louisiana
State University Press:* Parties, The Governor of
Desire, *and* On Long Mountain. *Ms. Morgan has
been the recipient of a National Endowment for the
Arts fellowship, the Emily Clarke Balch Award from
the* Virginia Quarterly Review, *and the Best
Screenplay Award from the Virginia Film Festival.*

Swing, Boat, Table

What Hanno has made of wood this year:
a swing, a boat, a table.

He doesn't believe he's made art this year;
the swing, the boat, the table

are objects he made to invite those he loves
to sit down.

Not objects people in rooms walk around,
regard in boredom or awe while locked at the knee—

a few vaguely yearning to float to the sea,
break bread with friends, rise through the air—

a few vaguely yearning—and not knowing why—
to sit in a tree.

At Epidaurus

Our little tribe
twenty or so
from the old New World
sat in a segment of curve
on the first two rows
of stone.

September had emptied
the ancient theater
cut into the pine groves
on Mount Kynortion,
though a summer sun
still burned down
from cloudless blue
over Mycenae and Argos,
over us.

We leaned into each other
for shade and to listen
to the one man among us
who knew the old words.

Alone in the center
of the packed-earth round,
he recited the poetry
of Euripides:
the longing of Phaedra
to be right and do wrong—
though nobody, not
even the guides from Nauplia,
knew that Greek
that struck passion
on reason like match
on stone.

Still,
unruly children
got quiet.
A few tourists testing
the famous acoustics,
even two stonecutters
at work by the exit
(listening to rock
on a yellow radio)
grew quiet

as his unintelligible words
flickered into rhythm
then rose like the flame
from Olympus
one runner keeps lit.

While around us,
behind us
across the sun-struck stage
the empty stone rows
ranged up to the sky like years

strictly attending to what
they've come down to.

Debra Nystrom

Debra Nystrom's first book, A Quarter Turn, *was published by Sheep Meadow Press in 1991, and her second,* Torn Sky, *will be published by Sarabande Books in 2003. She has been a Hoyns Fellow in Poetry at the University of Virginia and a recipient of a Virginia Commission for the Arts prize. Born in South Dakota in 1954, Ms. Nystrom is a graduate of the Goddard Writing Program, and she currently teaches creative writing at the University of Virginia. She has twice received* Shenandoah's *James Boatwright Prize for Poetry.*

Peggy Harrison

The Cliff Swallows

Is it some turn of wind
that funnels them all down at once, or
is it their own voices netting
to bring them in—the roll and churr
of hundreds searing through river light
and cliff dust, each to its precise
mud nest on the face—
none of our own isolate
groping, wishing need could be sent
so unerringly to solace. But
this silk-skein flashing is like heaven
brought down: not to meet ground
or water, but to enter
the riven earth and disappear.

Emily's Ghost

Sumac tassels shrivel at their tips,
the milkweed hulls have all cracked open—
only this one I've found with a few seeds left,
their fibers still waiting for the wind.

I push up a sleeve and blow them myself
down my bare arm
and one white veil snags in the ragged bouquet
that has my hand sweating and stinking of weed-balm:

Queen Anne's lace and these strange
prickly purple berries.
They make a lovely arrangement,
and as long as I have the bouquet to carry,

the trucks and pickups bumping by
flashing sun off their windshields into my eyes
should see no need to honk or hoot or pull over
to offer a ride. At least no need of mine.

Trisha Orr

Gregory Orr

*Gregory Orr was born in Albany, New York, in 1947
and now teaches in the M.F.A. program at the
University of Virginia. He is the author of* Richer
Entanglements: Essays and Notes on Poetry and
Poems *(University of Michigan 1993), as well as
many collections of poems, including* The Caged
Owl: New and Selected Poems *(2002) and*
Orpheus and Eurydice *(2001), both from Copper
Canyon Press;* Burning the Empty Nests *(Carnegie
Mellon University 1997); and* City of Salt *(University
of Pittsburgh 1995). A recipient of a Guggenheim
fellowship, two National Endowment for the Arts
fellowships, and a Rockefeller fellowship, Mr. Orr is
poetry editor of the* Virginia Quarterly Review.

Like Any Other Man

I was born with a knife
in one hand
and a wound in the other.

In the house where I lived
all the mirrors
were painted black.

So many years
before the soft key of your tongue
unlocked my body.

Leaving the Asylum

The metal harps of the high gates
make a clangorous music
closing behind me. They
announce the "new life" of freedom

and only a battered valise
to lug down this alley of poplars.
I repeat the litany of the poem
that released me.
                    Hollow tree
though I am, these things I cherish:
the hum of my blood, busily safe
in its hive of being; the delicate
oily kiss my fingertips give
each thing they touch; and desire,
a huge fish I drag with me
through the wilderness:
I love its glint among the dust and stones.

We Must Make a Kingdom of It

So that a colony will breed here,
love rubs together two words:
"I" and "she." How the long bone
of the personal pronoun
warms its cold length against her fur.
                    *
She plants the word "desire"
that makes the very air
amorous, that causes the light,
from its tall stalk, to bend down
until it almost kisses the ground.
                    *
It was green, I saw it—tendril
flickering from dry soil
like a grass snake's tongue;
call it "flame"—light
become life, what the word
wants, what the earth
in its turning
yearns for: to writhe and rise up,
even to fly briefly

like the shovelful over
the gravedigger's shoulder.

Celestial Desolations

Glitter and gone—
is that wrong?
To shatter
then vanish?

What if the heart
lacks alchemy,
can't pearl
its hurt, can't
turn it nacreous?

And how can we know
the lute will leap
from the beautiful wound?

Eric Pankey

*Eric Pankey lives in Fairfax, Virginia, and teaches
English at George Mason University. Born in Kansas
City, Missouri, in 1959, Mr. Pankey received his
education at the University of Missouri and the
University of Iowa. His first book of poems,* For the
New Year, *won the Walt Whitman Award in 1984. He
has since published* Heartwood *(Atheneum 1988)
and* Apocrypha *(1991),* The Late Romances *(1997),
and* Cenotaph *(2000), all from Knopf. Mr. Pankey
has received grants from the Ingram-Merrill
Foundation and the National Endowment for the
Arts; his work has also appeared in the* Kenyon
Review *and* Verse.

Nostalgia

Afterward, it was hard to sleep at night
With only the hiss of the possum
And the mole's dull progress to fill the stillness.

The owl's talons closed too quietly on the vole.
After rain, wind brought down the rain in the trees,
But neither a storm nor the *drip, drip* repaired

The material of experience,
The unmendable rent of what is withheld.
What is the Word that it remains silent

Here in the impasse after creation,
Where he wakes, startled by a voice, and awake
Finds his own mouth formed around an unsayable word?

Crab Apple

The thin chipped branches of the crab apples
      are as hard as anything
    that holds on beneath the iron cast
      of late autumn sky.

Whoever planted them as ornament
      must have loved the scattered nest,
    the broken-knuckled look of the thing,
      must have loved the fruit,

the unripe pithy white, the dusty red,
      some speckled with mold, some pecked
    but not eaten, the holes edged with black,
      black like charred paper.

If the trees are bent it is not from fruit.
      Each year they shrink a little.
    The ground beneath them goes soft with rot.
      The bark grays like shale.

You can only eat so much sour jam,
      and when you do you are left
    with the cramped, twisted look of the trees,
      a look so jagged,

you almost forget the season they flower.

A Walk with My Father

A columbine's clear violet after noon rain.

The ditch of a creek we'd followed here,
muddy water stippled with shadow. It is 1966.
On the bank, a carp, or what was left of one,

covered with a glow of flies. Green, gold,
a momentary body of light
lifted as he turned the fish over with a stick.

The exposed flesh was flat, white,
raw as wound. Unearthly.
Or too much of the earth:

the dull texture of clay, the dust white of lime.

To satisfy me, he pushed it over the grassy bank.
The heat was visible on the rank air,
rising against a drift of daisies.

I followed the fish downstream until it caught on rocks
—pale jutted limestone, and the slow water
worked its gill. Opening, open, as if that would help.

Jim Peterson

Jim Peterson is a professor and coordinator of creative writing at Randolph-Macon Woman's College. Mr. Peterson was born in Augusta, Georgia, in 1948. His recent books include the chapbook Greatest Hits 1984–2000 *(Pudding House 2001) and the collections* The Owning Stone *(Red Hen 2000) and* An Afternoon with K *(Holocene 1996). Mr. Peterson won the 1999 Benjamin Saltman Award and has published work in* Shenandoah *and the* Georgia Review.

Fish to Fry

An unsolved murder, a flock of thieves
circling the city among pigeons, a bomb
threat and the real thing raining debris
into the streets, these are the fish fried
in the same pan day after day. And if
the young girl escapes the rapist's grasp,
plunging into the shocked headlights
of a busy road, her story is thrown
back into the pond of her own dreams,
a shark lurking among the bass and bream.
But if she disappears for days, if her
body is found in the woods, every drop
of the spirit squeezed out of her like
water from a new sponge, flash-bulbs
sprout up around her like magic tulips,
voices crawl into her wounds like insects,
the hands of white-coated men break her
further open like so much suspicious fruit.
It is the clues they want, the innuendoes
of brutality, of the final bursting into
flames of her desire to live. Next day,
we will feed upon her as the killer fed,

our eyes moving from column to column
like the wild boar's snout over ground.
By afternoon, her story will be fit
kindling for the evening fire, fit
wrapping for the last lucky catch at dusk.

Not Talking at Dawn

He stands in the mouth of his garage
with a pine board in his hands.
Morning light etches the details
of his neighbor's porch rail and shutters
and the white mortar between bricks,
the sublunar landscape of pine bark
awaking to the traffic of ants and lizards
and those small jumping spiders with big eyes.
He rises early in order to get more done
and he would say something about that
but getting more done is only yesterday's dream,
and no one is listening. He sands a board
and applies the first coat for another
shelf in the basement, loving the smell
of that dark walnut stain. He feels
a familiar stillness burning into the slow
unfolding of his nerves, into the long
loosening of his joints like the way the stain
heightens the fluid grain of this common pine,
feels the steady adhesion of his jaw, teeth
settling into their perfect fit.
As he lays the board in its place—
he will drive the nails tomorrow—
he wonders what teeth and bones
would have to say if left to themselves.
He remembers the skull his science teacher
brought into class years ago, turning it carefully
so everyone could see, pointing out

the parietal, occipital and temporal bones,
probing the foramen magnum with two fingers.
He remembers the heft of it in his own hands,
how awake it seemed without flesh,
without tongue or voice.

Hermine Pinson

Born in east Texas, Hermine Pinson is a professor of African American literature at the College of William and Mary. She is the author of two volumes of poetry, Mamma Yetta *(1999) and* Ashe *(1992), both from Wings Press, and one play,* Walk Together, Children. *Ms. Pinson has also published work in* Common Bonds *and* Callaloo.

Left-Handed Poem

Left hand turns inward
then rises like an ominous
hump from the limp neck
of the wrist
when I am making a point
or begging
          to differ
fingers and thumb poised
to pick up some subtle thing
                    beyond themselves
came out of the womb that way
left hand turned inward
hard against the heart
transparent knuckles
but workers' hands
          like Papa Johnny's
came out that way and
          almost broke my arm
the doctor pushed me back in again
so I could come out
right
in sleep the back of the hand
is half-closed against
                    the sheets
tending a dreamer's chores or

guarding against
some slight
imagined or otherwise
I used to play saxophone
Now I press fingers to soundless keys
the task:
      reach through the space on the page
for some subtle thing
half-turning motion of pincers
      in the ocean of heartways—
at rest the left hand lies:
      a failed balletic exercise
an invalid's carelessness
a pulse
a time signature
      a womb's knowledge
of life's ceaseless motion.

Lucinda Roy

Larry Jackson

Born in 1955, Lucinda Roy was raised in London, England, and received her education from King's College and the University of Arkansas. Ms. Roy is currently the Alumni Distinguished Professor in English and director of creative writing at Virginia Tech. In addition to her poetry collection, The Humming Birds, *which won the 1994 Eighth Mountain Poetry Prize, Ms. Roy has published two novels,* Lady Moses *and* The Hotel Alleluia. *Her work has appeared in* American Poetry Review *and* Shenandoah.

The Curtsy

The trouble was that Anna's curtsy was a kind of defecation.

Whenever she lowered herself down into the dirt
she took you with her into shit
and left you there.
It wasn't mannerly.
It made pale women light up with fury;
it made ruddy men shift from one leg to the other
as if a slave had caught them
in an act of bestiality.

Even after they lopped off her ears
(Mr. Ellis once or twice recalled they fell to the stable floor
like scarlet petals and lay there for fifteen minutes before the
dogs came in) she still imbued her curtsies with a curse.

Old Ellis decided to let it be.
There was only so much a man could do
to render a woman impotent.
He told his guests she was something of a spitfire
and focused on the biscuits she made—the best
this side of the Mississippi, he boasted.

And after the women left, he'd add:
"These biscuits slip down your throat like the tongue of a whore."
And the men would nod, knowing precisely what he meant.

The Virginia Reel

In nineteen ninety-four, the plantation
hums with tourists; the slave quarters are full
of whimsy. It is fall. The leaves are scarlet.
The guide points out the cabins as they lean
into winter. He whips us into frenzy—
the banquets, the gardens, the cooks, the maids,
the butlers, the grandeur, the books, the balls—
always the balls. Women dancing like girls,
in corsets tight as fists; men, heady with
perfume, ready to die for a kiss.
Outside the trees are on fire. It is fall.
Inside the enormous house a staircase
defies the laws of gravity, suspended
from the landing like a Bible vision.
We say half-jokingly it cannot hold us.
It does, in spite of logic. We talk
about the years it took to build those stairs.
Our guide is close to tears as he caresses
smooth brown wood.
We hold on to the railing. We could fall,
all of us together, if the structure
doesn't hold. We climb. It holds. We shake
our heads and laugh. Laughter takes us
into double-barreled spirals, a falling
into where we were before.

                    It is fall
and hoops and petticoats sweep the master's house,
and Lucy carries the mistress' chamber pot
softly down the stairs. Rawhide shoes
(greased with tallow so they slip right on)

make the workers quiet. Yesterday a man
stood up and flew home.
Mary witnessed it, so did Rebecca,
Hester, and Prince Josiah. Not like birds,
they say, but like leaves raised up by whirlwinds,
Elijah the Fool flew on home. Too dumb
to grow wings, Hester says, the poor fool screamed
and tried to cling to her headtie. But no one cheats
the Lord. Elijah stole her red headtie.
Hester wants it back. In the fields, dreaming
is dangerous. Hester is whipped for staring
at a cardinal. "Birds is birds," the foreman
says to her. That night they gather in a flock
of hope and stand where the Fool had stood. Nothing.
No one remembers the words that brought them
here. Elijah knew them. Hummed
the songs he had the words to. Never shared
a damn thing. But catch him unawares and hear
something wild coming from his throat. The same
sound he made when the whirlwind took him up
and spun him round like cotton on a spool and
flung him up into the sky above their heads.
Elijah's clothes tore off his back, his shirt
waved to them before it fluttered down.
Prince Josiah wears it now and stands there
in the spot where foolery had stood and nothing happens.
Mary blinks her one remaining eye
in the dark and thinks she hears a sound
like white folks' clothes swishing up the leaves.
"Ghosts!" she cries and scurries into dark
with all the rest. Lucy thinks about the Fool.
Up in the air it is quiet. She knows
the tops of trees. Brought late into this world,
she still recalls the other. She has brown scraps
sewn together in a band to match
her stolen children's skins. She knows water
in a river and the green of leaves
a deeper green than southern green; and she

remembers names for places and names for friends
and names for when they took her out of breathing
into wood. She mumbles something close
to prayer, holding the chamber pot away
from her skirt as she winds down the spiral
staircase. He flew! She will conjure up words
again, and see if she can call the wind
the way Elijah did, wrap it round
her body like a coat, and fly back
to the light of ancient rivers. In the wake
of flight, she hums songs taught her by her
mother's mothers.

                The music room is oval
like an egg. The guide points out the rounded
hearths and mantels; curved glass echoes the mistress'
harp and violin. "Harmony," he says,
"the great quest for harmony lives in the walls
of this house." People nod. (Beneath the stairs
the swish of muck in chamber pots and Lucy's
hum, suspended in the sweet Virginia breeze,
riding the updraft of air like flame.)

Sarah Huntington

Steve Scafidi

*Steve Scafidi was born in Loudoun County,
Virginia, in 1967. He earned his B.A. at Virginia
Commonwealth University and his M.F.A. at Arizona
State University. Mr. Scafidi received a grant from
the Virginia Commission for the Arts, and his first
book,* Sparks from a Nine-Pound Hammer, *was
published by Louisiana State University Press in
2001. His work has appeared in the* Southern
Review, American Poetry Review, *and* Prairie
Schooner. *He currently works as a cabinetmaker
in Purcellville, Virginia.*

On Looking into Golding's Ovid

It's still the same—he turns, she turns—the end
of a candle burns, maybe, in the eye socket
of a severed head. It's still the same wedding
guests who fill these straw canoes, who float
downriver swinging their lamps and calling
out for the groom. Orpheus is still mostly soil
splashing onto soil where the maenads squat.

Maybe a shepherd found a head and carved
the wet face from the white bone and now
dreams some strange version—a candle
glowing in his little room—of an early home.
It's still the same. Eurydice is cold or alone.
Or both. What if she ran ahead, long ago,
and overtook that man she loved, on the path.

What if she brushed quietly past him, and then
she looked back? I'm tired of stories of the asp,
and the wish of little wings where a god turns.
It's still the same. Every night, those revelers
calling from the water. I'd like to believe she

found a way out of the earth one night and then
reversed all that happened—I'd like to believe

she is wearing a wool shirt with tiny white buttons
along the arms, and that we have four children
who never visit and we eat long ornate meals
together in perfect happiness and everything
we ever wanted is ours for the asking and that
she would please quiet those strangers on the river.
It's still the same—he turns, she turns—story that burns.

To Whoever Set My Truck on Fire

But let us be friends awhile and understand our differences
are small and that they float like dust in sunny rooms
and let us settle into the good work of being strangers
simply who have something to say in the middle of the night
for you have said something that interests me—something
    of flames,

footsteps and the hard heavy charge of an engine gunning away
into the June cool of four in the morning here in West Virginia
where last night I woke to the sound of a door slamming,
five or six fading footsteps, and through the window saw
my impossible truck bright orange like a maverick sun and

ran—I did—panicked in my underwear bobbling the dumb
extinguisher too complex it seemed for putting out fires
and so grabbed a skillet and jumped about like one
needing to piss while the faucet like honey issued its slow
sweet water and you I noticed then were watching

from your idling car far enough away I could not make
your plate number but you could see me—half naked
figuring out the puzzle of a fire thirty seconds from

a dream never to be remembered while the local chaos
of a growing fire crackled through the books and boots

burning in my truck, you bastard, you watched as I sprayed
finally the flames with a gardenhose under the moon
and yes I cut what was surely a ridiculous figure there
and worsened it later that morning after the bored police
drove home lazily and I stalked the road in front of my house

with an ax in my hand and walked into the road after
every car to memorize the plates of who might have done this:
LB 7329, NT 7663, and you may have passed by—
I don't know—you may have passed by as I committed
the innocent numbers of neighbors to memory and maybe

you were miles away and I, like the woodsman of fairy tales,
threatened all with my bright ax shining with the evil
joy of vengeance and mad hunger to bring harm—heavy
harm—to the coward who did this and if I find you,
my friend, I promise you I will lay the sharp blade deep

into your body until the humid grabbing hands of what must be
death have mercy and take you away from the constant
murderous swinging my mind makes my words make
swinging down on your body and may your children
weep a thousand tears at your small and bewildered grave.

Ode to Rosa Parks

In the forests of Alabama where pine trees crowd the air and scrape
        the blue sky raw and heat sifts down a few degrees
where green moss creeps on stones and crawls over the earth,

I will bet all I ever loved that just below the surface here you will find
        the bones of men smashed by roots and the gray rinds
of the skulls of women broken open like sudden storms one at a time

over the brutal southern course of years and you could populate
            three or four medium-sized towns with the bodies lost
in the forests outside Montgomery Alabama and forty-five years of

clear starry nights have passed over these pines since that afternoon
            in December 1955 when you risked the sudden
rage of whites who mobbed up at a moment's notice and the
    midnight

cruelties of Alabama were practiced so well so often that the
    smallest
            act of defiance was a matter of life and death and you
did not move to the back of the bus as you were told to and it was

dangerous, always dangerous, to have any courage in the South,
            just to open your mouth, or to breathe in and out,
and you did not move to the back of that bus on Cleveland Avenue,

Secretary of an Alabama chapter of the NAACP, Lady Courageous,
            Rosa Parks, sitting in that seat you saved us
the difficult sweet word *free.*

Nancy Schoenberger

Nancy Schoenberger's 1987 collection Girl on a
White Porch *received the Devins Award from the
University of Missouri Press, and her third collection
of poems,* Long like a River, *was awarded the 1997
Poetry Prize from New York University Press. Born in
1950 in Oakland, California, Ms. Schoenberger lives
in Williamsburg, Virginia. She has held fellowships
from the National Endowment for the Arts and
the Virginia Commission for the Arts, and she is
currently an associate professor of creative writing at
the College of William and Mary. In 2001 Doubleday
published her* Dangerous Muse: The Life of Lady
Caroline Blackwood. *Ms. Schoenberger is also
senior editor of the poetry journal* Verse.

Nathaniel Hawthorne in Hell

Is it what you imagined—not fires
but an icy mist, and a river where
you dipped your hand once, freezing it
to the wrist, the pierced veil

still clinging to your face? The others
are shrouded, though they call each
to each to pull down the bandages
masking their faces: Do you know

what it was like? Sophia's crossed over,
and Alymer, and even Dorcus—the ghosts
of your imagination, set free to
pick through the shards of your experiments,

among hosts of boys who released their souls
at Antietam, at Shiloh, and Manassas—
their limbs blown into the Indian woods
on the smoking banks of the Chickahominy.

Long like a River

I wonder what happened to my poor dog's soul.
I see her swimming through a muddy river—
silvered, dense, fluorescent—her neck and shoulders
serious with intention. But what river?
St. Johns River running thickly by my parents'
fallen mansion, from the fallen days of our childhood
in billowing Florida? (Garfish washed up
on the sandbagged lip of shore, where lolling
manatees once combed their hair, and Father shot
cartridges at an alligator, dense and buoyant
as a log, that logged its voyage past
our house on St. Johns bay, on its way
through suburbs to some ancient ooze.) The Miss-
ississippi? Long as its Indian name, it poured through
St. Louis where my grandmother grew, an Irish girl
green as its green banks and the tea she brewed
for her father and mother, who buried their hands
in her waist-length red hair. Long like the river
that runs to New Orleans, and further south
to the south of Buras, Louisiana,
its luxuries of oranges, its natural gasses
and convocations of fanciful insects? Here's where
a father learned how to gamble, and shoot small game,
and mow a long-haired field and harvest crawfish,
the length of any river like the length of a life
remembered when the mind refuses to go forward.
What are the words for the rivers we love?
The Clark Fork, snow-fed, its full house
of trout the dream of a summer noon? Plentiful,
ice-cold, the color of rusted tin? Is this
where a dog can swim to some animal heaven,
this river, swim beyond the shame of allegiance
to an alien tribe, a capricious master,
in the arms of some heavenly river?

Tim Seibles

*Norfolk resident Tim Seibles has published five
volumes of poetry, including* Hammerlock (1999)
and Hurdy-Gurdy (1992), *both from Cleveland
State University Press. Born in Philadelphia in 1955
and educated at Vermont College, Mr. Seibles has
been a National Endowment for the Arts fellow and
the recipient of an Open Voice Award. Mr. Seibles has
taught at Antioch University Southern California
and is now an associate professor in the M.F.A.
program at Old Dominion University. His work
has recently been published in* New Letters *and
the* Progressive.

Latin

Words slip into a language the way
white-green vines slide between slats in a fence.

A couple opens the door to a restaurant,
sees the orange and black colors everywhere

and the waitress grins, "Yeah,
a little Halloween overkill, huh."

Overkill, a noun for all of us
fidgeting under the nuclear umbrella—

but for that instant it just meant too many decorations,
too many paper skeletons and hobgobbled balloons.

———

I know a woman who is tall with dark hair,
who makes me think of honeysuckle

whenever she opens her legs. Not just the flower
but the dew-soaked music itself   *honeysuckle* like a flavor.

And I remember the first time years back
when LaTina told me what it was we had

between our eight-year-old front teeth
that April afternoon, our hands wet

with rain from the vines. "Honey sickle," she said,
while the white flower bloomed from the side of her mouth,

and I had a new sweetness on my tongue and a word
I'd never heard before. How was it decided in the beginning?

This word   for *this* particular thing,
a sound attached to a shape or feeling forever.

———————

All summer long the cicadas don't know
what we call them.

They sneak from the ground every year after dark,
break out of their shells right into the language,

and it holds them like a net made of nothing
but the need to make strange things familiar.

All summer long they rattle trees like maracas
until they become part of our weather—

quiet in rain, crazy in hard sun,
so we say *those cicadas sure make enough noise, huh.*

And the noise of that sentence   heard ten-thousand times
becomes a name for *us* the cicadas keep trying to say.

———————

I think about dying sometimes,
not the sudden death in the movies—

the red hole in the shirt, the eyes
open like magazines left on a waiting room table—

not that, but withering slowly like a language,
barely holding on until everything

I ever did or said   is just gone, absorbed
into something I would never have imagined—

like Latin. Not lost completely, but moved away
from that bright, small place

between seeing   and naming,
between the slow roll of ocean

and the quick intake of air
that would fill the word *wave.*

Dana Littlepage Smith

Richmond native Dana Littlepage Smith's first book,
Women Clothed with the Sun, *was published by*
Louisiana State University Press in 2001. Born
in 1963, she was educated at Brown University,
Virginia Commonwealth University, and Princeton
University. Ms. Smith has won various poetry prizes
in both the United States and the United Kingdom
and currently lives in Exeter, England. She is a
writing tutor at Strode College.

Asherah

> The women knead their dough, to make cakes
> to the Queen of Heaven.
> —Jer. 7:18

When pine splintered and the moon
scuttled down the mouth of a pitch pool,

I dived neat as pike & spoke to the unborn Christ.
"Bone faithful I'll be. Heaven's Other, if you like—

On that day, let the dead bury the dead.
Leave devils to pitch themselves off cliffs like swine.

Our limbs could grow lean & light.
We'll swallow night on night of clove-spiced wine."

Then the Ghost of him, all Holy, yawned.
I saw the stars wheel in its mouth.

Don't tell me what it means to be the apple
of some God's eye, his turtledove,

safe & fat beneath the eaves.
The day the rich go empty-handed

and the poor belch honey and cream,
I'll let my iced love flood

by tides, until it waxes blue,
then silver, wanes.

The Widow and Her Mite

> And Jesus said, "This widow has cast in more
> than all the rich, for she has given all the
> living that she had."
> —Luke 21:3−4

Two thousand years and still the question begs,
Why did I do it? The sky rained no fire.
No asses sang hosannas when I walked by.
Though I saw the temple beggar sucking
his single coin as if it were a loaf of bread.
He spat when I passed him, his voice thinned
by poverty to a thread of hammered iron.
The indigo dark eyes of justice neither blinked
nor looked away when I dropped my two mites
into the coffer. I didn't eat that night.
Nor did I count myself amongst the blessed.

The dread of want had dogged me so many days
that when the coins fell I heard nothing:
the nothing that I had to lose.

They called me the crazed widow
with pinwheel eyes until the words of Christ
rebuked them. Then elders bought me azure skirts
and claimed I'd walked the flaming maze

of Yahweh's mind. Now when crowds gather
to hear my story, I keep it spare:

Why wear the crow-footed face
of fear? What is a mite?
Who is this widow talking?

Dave Smith

Dave Smith was born in Portsmouth, Virginia, in 1942 and attended the University of Virginia. For many years, he taught English at Louisiana State University, where he was coeditor of the Southern Review *and* Louisiana State University Press, *and he now teaches at Johns Hopkins University. His many books of poems include* Cumberland Station, Homage to Edgar Allan Poe, In the House of the Judge, Fate's Kite, *and* The Wick of Memory: New and Selected Poems. *He has received awards and fellowships from the National Endowment for the Arts, the Guggenheim Foundation, and the Rockefeller Foundation, and has edited several books of criticism.*

Night Pleasures

Poquoson, Virginia

Where I come from land lies flat as paper.
       Pine, spruce, holly like dark words
left from a woods. Creeks coil, curve,
       enigmatic as women. To know the depths
you must dream. In the mountains
       for college I walked up and could see
barns, cows, housesmoke, but no boats.
       Hillsides of apples, still, perfect.

Here my little boat takes the night Bay.
       One far neon light tosses, a city
people walk alone, its rhythmic
       landscape cut from marshes and cries.
On black water it is all mine, first
       beginnings, endings, love's beauties.
So when I move, it moves under me, and knows me.

Canary Weather in Virginia

It comes in sharp, salt smell above James River's foam.
It clatters past azalea, willow, the exhumed sway
Of laurel, camellia's pink-smoked buds dawning open,
Oiling a woman's hands to spill moonlight in woe's rooms.
It flings unseen to anywhere he lives bands of wind
Unfolding so many gold birds dawn sings with god-breath.
Yellow-red streaks pass like her hair over his pillow.
What mission has it in droughty fields, uncoiling faith
That remembers to bring also cardinals, owls, gulls?
Swamp-sheen, a dew-gilt mast, mullet's leap, cold horse-eye
Lift, hold him up, though he stiffens, alone in his yard.
When tides wash distance in, he floats, fate's kite, back
To silhouettes of pine, boats, that whirling yellow bird.

Crab House

Noon at the swamp's heart, the stink
falling from the smokestacks
cloaking the slender reeds that do not move.

Workboat's kapucka-kapucka pushes
the dark wave in over the mud,
then pulls it back so the skulls shine.

A gull settles onto a distant swell,
picks at white feathers like a German maid
in a sun-dappled bed. The sound of many legs

scraping against metal, the sound of water
boiling is in this air. I listen
as the swamp grinds its teeth, feeds, begins to reek.

On a Field Trip at Fredericksburg

The big steel tourist shield says maybe
fifteen thousand got it here. No word
of either Whitman or one uncle
I barely remember in the smoke
that filled his tiny mountain house.

If each finger were a thousand of them
I could clap my hands and be dead
up to my wrists. It was quick
though not so fast as we can do it
now, one bomb, atomic or worse,
the tiny pod slung on wingtip,
high up, an egg cradled
by some rapacious mockingbird.

Hiroshima canned nine times their number
in a flash. Few had the time
to moan or feel the feeling
ooze back in the groin.

In a ditch I stand
above Marye's Heights, the bookish
faces of Brady's fifteen-year-old
drummers, before battle, rigid
as August's dandelions
all the way to the Potomac
rolling in my skull.

If Audubon came here, the names
of birds would gush, the marvel
single feathers make
evoke a cloud, a nation,
a gray blur preserved
on a blue horizon, but
there is only a wandering child,
one dark stalk snapped off

in her hand. Hopeless teacher,
I take it, try to help her
hold its obscure syllables
one instant in her mouth,
like a drift of wind
at the forehead, the front door,
the black, numb fingernails.

Near the Docks

There was a fire in the night.
Across the street I slept among the others
as the ash snowed upon small pines.
I slept owning nothing, a child ignorant
of fortune's blistering story, the playful
flash in the dark, the unseen smolder
that would leave us revealed, though
unchanged as the black earth.
I said my prayers for luck
like the man trying to live
in two houses, hoping for time
to leave the old one of his fathers,
its windows with weariness fogged.
The other was half-built, roofless,
green timbers going gray in sun
like a vision that would not be done.

I had climbed there all summer to smoke
after the hours when I would find him
hunched on his wooden stool. Each
morning, halfway between the houses,
on his tongue would be the story
of how they came and of the sea,
his hands weaving wire to a trap,
making careful seams to catch
cunning scuttlers. I saw his wife
already had begun to hang her wash,

its shapes rueful, steaming, ghostly
in sunflare. That day a mongrel
lapped from the ruts of the fire trucks.

I thought little was changed by fire,
only his toolshed limp as a black sail
left in a heap, and that new hole
in the landscape. This was a poor place
where no one came, luckless, desperate,
eternal as guilt. I was the same
as the day before. In silence
I greeted that old one. Now I remember
seeing also, as if for the first time,
the shocking gray face of the sea
was his, fixed, in one quick glance.
It loomed up human and beautiful
as far off the figures of boats
crossed, worked, and seemed to sink
while they burned in the sullen sun.

Of Oystermen, Workboats

The wide, white, wing-boned washboards of twenty
footers, sloped, ridged to hold
a man's tongs and stride,

                the good stance
to scrape deep with a motion like big applause,
plunging the teeth true beyond the known
mounds of the dead, the current carried
cloisters of murk,
            miracles that bloom
luminous and unseen, sweet things to be
brought up, bejeweled, culled from husks,

as oystermen like odd angels glide far off enough
to keep a wake gentle as shirts on a line,

red baseball caps dipping like bloodied
heads upright, the clawed hands slapped
at the air in salute,

                  those washboards that splinter
the sun on tongs downlaid, on tines humming,

those womb-hulls harbored flank to flank at dusk
until the white-robed priest of the moon
stands tall to the sea's spume-pour
in nostrils
           of the men who sway from heel to heel,

the season come again, the socketed gray
of their eyes rolling outward,
forearms naked past longjohns,
the salted breast-beaters at first light

lined up, ready to fly.

R. T. Smith

*Born in Washington, D.C., in 1947, Rod Smith
currently edits* Shenandoah *for Washington and
Lee University. He was raised in North Carolina and
Georgia and educated at the University of North
Carolina—Charlotte and Appalachian State
University. He has received fellowships from the
National Endowment for the Arts and state arts
agencies in Virginia and Alabama. His books include*
Brightwood *(2003),* Messenger *(2001), and*
Trespasser *(1995), all from Louisiana State
University Press, and* The Hollow Log Lounge
*(University of Illinois 2003). He received the Library
of Virginia Poetry Book of the Year Award in 2002.*

Alphabet

In the sewing room
the mail-order Singer
with its chrome-rimmed
wheel and gleaming needle
was turned under
to make a desk while
mother started dinner.

I faced west where
the window shimmered.
For an hour I rehearsed
my letters, spelling
everything visible—
zipper and scissors,
thimbles and spools.
The oval mirror made
the wallpaper zinnias
flower still further,
and a mantel clock
held the minutes back.

The Eagle pencil
in my cramped hand
scratched fishhook
j or an *l* like a needle.
Late sunlight glazed
the holly leaves silver
beyond the peeling sill.
While I squinted hard
at the Blue Horse paper,
the twilight world
held perfectly still.

When I was finished,
each curve and flourish
set in disciplined rows,
fresh tea with ice
appeared at my elbow,
the yellow *c* of lemon
in the tumbler's perfect *o*,
and if mother had praise
for what I had done,
I would shine all evening
bright as a straight pin,
while the new moon
with its careless serifs
cleared the trees and rose.

Zion, Vernacular Exposure, Mockingbird Song

I won't forget the museum—it was in Mississippi,
it was winter, snow covering the pastures
like cotton never could—and the photographs

in black and white by a local amateur shutterbug
with an unerring eye covered an off-white wall,
the grainy prints framed with minimal chrome.

The wind outside was wild, something out of Job,
which seemed right, its white-out affliction
of window just beside the largest portrait.

Hair like spangle-ice and five o'clock frost
grizzling his face, a black granddaddy dressed
in hospital whites leaned forward in the wicker seat

of his ladder-back chair and stared into the pages
of a Bible wide open in his lap. I could see
the spine was broken, pages ragged and thin

as Kleenex. His lips were half open in a whisper,
as if giving breath to the scripture, warming
that wilderness of sticks the alphabet cools to

when no one's there to witness. I hope I'll always
remember to love that shine the sunlight
and an inch of Tri-X film caught in his old eyes—

grace radiant, as if he'd seen angels in silver
spread their wings. The caption chosen
by the camera man or curator

was "Cramming for the Finals," which left me
weak-kneed and hearing my grandma's soprano
reach from "blessed assurance" to "glory divine"

with her small-town Georgia drawl, while
snowflakes like words of a hesitant holy message
whirled beyond the panes. Now, just drifting,

looking up from the Dell laptop balanced across
my knees and trying to think beyond thinking,
I see March manna blowing in huge tatters

above the yellow flowers, and the orchard
mockingbird shivers, extends one wing's
extravagance of white and pewter to sing what,

as we still say down here—because the vernacular
is what the oracle trusts to heat the alphabet up—
might could be my name.

Scavenging the Wall

When fall brought the graders to Atlas Road,
I drove through gray dust thick as a battle
and saw the ditch freshly scattered with gravel.

Leveling, shaving on the bevel, the blade
and fanged scraper had summoned sleepers—
limestone loaves and blue slate, skulls of quartz

not even early freeze had roused. Some rocks
were large as buckets, others just a scone
tumbled up and into light for the first time

in ages. Loose, sharp, they were a hazard
to anyone passing. So I gathered
what I could, scooped them into the bed

and trucked my freight away under birdsong
in my own life's autumn. I was eager
to add to the snaggled wall bordering

my single acre, to be safe, to be still
and watch the planet's purposeful turning
behind a cairn of roughly balanced stones.

Uprooted, scarred, weather-gray of bones,
I love their old smell, the familiar unknown.
To be sure this time I know where I belong

I have brought, at last, the vagrant road home.

Ron Smith

*Ron Smith, born in 1949 in Savannah, Georgia,
lives in Richmond, Virginia, where he is chairman
of the English department at St. Christopher's School.
He has also taught at the University of Richmond,
Virginia Commonwealth University, and Mary
Washington College. His book of poetry,* Running
Again in Hollywood Cemetery, *was published by
the University Presses of Florida in 1988. He received
the 1986 Guy Owen Prize from the* Southern Poetry
Review *and has been a Roper Graduate Fellow in
English and a Bread Loaf Scholar in Poetry.*

Leaving Forever

My son can look me level in the eyes now,
and does, hard, when I tell him he cannot watch
chainsaw murders at the midnight movie,
that he must bend his mind to Biology,
under this roof, in the clear light of a Tensor lamp.
Outside, his friends throb with horsepower
under the moon.

        He stands close, milk sour
on his breath, gauging the heat of my conviction,
eye-whites pink from his new contacts.
He can see me better than before. And I can see
myself in those insolent eyes, mostly head
in the pupil's curve, closed in by the contours
of his unwrinkled flesh.

        At the window he waves
a thin arm and his buddies squall away in a glare
of tail lights. I reach out my hand to his shoulder,
but he shrugs free and shows me my father's narrow eyes,
the trembling hand at my throat, the hard wall
at the back of my skull, the raised fist framed

in the bedroom window I had climbed through
at 3 A.M.

"If you hit me, I'll leave forever,"
I said. But everything was fine in a few days, fine.
"I would have come back," I said, "false teeth and all."
Now, twice a year after the long drive, in the yellow light
of the front porch, I breathe in my father's whiskey,
ask for a shot and see myself distorted in
his thick glasses, the two of us grinning,
as he holds me with both hands at arm's length.

Photograph of Jesse Owens at the Gun

Beneath a puff of white gunsmoke a man
the shade of cinders has risen
from between white lines
at an angle sharp with speed.
He is himself a thrust of angles:
one foot down, one hand reaching,
elbow, knee, the single bend at the waist,
all his flesh strung tight.

In the background row of pale blurred faces
these who appear to wear his colors
must be his teammates.
We can tell only that
they do not seem to cheer.
Behind them the tiers of Berlin
mass into gray clouds.

All the races of 1936 are stopped
inside this black frame.
The man whose captured body
pulls us to the wall
cannot reach the tape, his form

caught here in the rough shape
of the swastikas that fly in the corner.

Nothing moves, nothing changes.
We stare and stare.

—for DS, CK, and TH

Katherine Soniat

*Katherine Soniat, born in Washington, D.C., in 1942,
is an associate professor of English at Virginia Tech.
Her books of poems are* Alluvial *(Bucknell University
2001),* A Shared Life *(University of Iowa 1994),
and* Cracking Eggs *(University of Florida 1990).
Among her many awards are the Iowa Poetry Prize,
the Camden Poetry Prize, and the Virginia Prize for
Poetry. Ms. Soniat's work has been published in the*
Kenyon Review, River Styx, *and* TriQuarterly.

Apricots and Oranges

Across gulfs and oceans I flew,
sealed in space, the body thrust forward
faster than any princely navigator could have imagined.
One by one, the overheads in airline cabins descended.
Red lines crawled the maps,
our progress mercurial high above the water,
the drifted landmasses seemingly laced in,
reuniting.
        That path mocked me,
as though I were the one cut down by a terminal fever,
and not the three I'd lost within months:
the dead and their wide swaths of disorder.
                    The emptied closets,
each intimacy I lived through
until, pushed by their silence, I took to the air,
to stone villages by the sea where little street dogs nudged
and knew how to make it better,
their lives fitted out with companions as they trotted
from dawn markets to the all-night corner tavern.

Pressure

January eclipse of the moon,
blank wafer slipped into black over the mountains.

Turn of the year. Dark of our season.
Rain in a cockeyed southwind

mauls the white atmosphere,
drowning any scheme to set the world

right.
The barometer drops.

The contradictions stand,
mixed message of the foot-up-and-ready-

never-to-come-down heron.
One-legged elite so sure

the heart will hold and not stop
in such stillness.

A sleepy mind fills with fissures,
clash of the spheres. Winter chimes.

Sages say we're due for this crack,
that our clock has tocked itself to pieces;

offer first your little toe to the tiger
and be licked to your senses,

rain washing snow from the dark.

Lisa Russ Spaar

Lisa Russ Spaar lives in Charlottesville, where she teaches at the University of Virginia and administers the M.F.A. program in creative writing. Originally from New Jersey, where she was born in 1956, Ms. Spaar is the editor of Acquainted with the Night: Insomnia Poems *(Columbia University 2000) and the author of* Glass Town *(Red Hen 2000). Her work has also appeared in* Poetry, *the* Kenyon Review, *the* Virginia Quarterly Review, *and* Shenandoah. *In 2000 Ms. Spaar received a Rona Jaffe Award.*

Rapunzel at 14

I've watched this before, the winey rust,
the haze accumulating in woods spread below me.
It's as though I were a god,
spying on the world from the air—
except that in the tower's cellar-cool room
at my back, the chamber pot is full of blood
and flies.
                              What's happening
to my eyes, that I can see now
with hawk's clarity the smallest mouse
tunneling through field straw, feel the red river
of fox moving toward the thicket
of last grapes?

I hold my mouth open, teeth bared
to the wind. Vegetables rot

in my keeper's basket, as birds
wheel and hurtle through the tower,
liming the flags and sill.

The green world's absent, a terrible nostalgia.
Still, so **what** that the world is dying?
Nothing's ever fallen past my shoulders
that wasn't part of me.

April

Bridal skirts of weeping cherry,
jilted by recent rain,
and the chimerical plum along the median strip

are washed with pinkish
hallucinatory white, and a slick
oceanic light suggests everything:

the signs, the fickle, strobing traffic lamps
reflected in the street, the whoosh and wake of passing cars.
Wet birds that blow apart the lawns

with sudden rising. On such a day,
I feel forgiven, as though I had new need
to be, as though winter were a blame

I carried in me always,
dragged along the ground in babyhood,
lugged higher as I grew, a glacial fist

clenching and unclenching inside
its neighborhood of bone and gristle.
The loopy signature of telephone wires

transmits inaudibly above; clouds break open.
Fresh draperies of pollen. My tires grip the gravel drive
that popples like another shore

and, turning the wheel, I find
I'm home, my armpits darkly sweet
with this sudden thaw that floods

my throat, my palms,
my nose, my eyes with helpless,
senseless absolution.

Dan Stryk

Dan Stryk, born in London, England, in 1951, has lived in Bristol, Virginia, for fifteen years. He is a professor of world literature and creative writing at Virginia Intermont College and is the author of Taping Images to Walls *(Pecan Grove 2001),* Death of a Sunflower *(Timberline 1999), and* The Artist and the Crow *(Purdue University 1984). Mr. Stryk has received a National Endowment for the Arts fellowship and an Illinois Arts Council grant. His work has appeared in* TriQuarterly, Southwest Review, *and* Tricycle: The Buddhist Review.

Spirit of Komodo

Craggy island lizard
    whose unblinking
eyes would hold mine
    for that brief
yet timeless moment
    through draped palm
fronds, belly swaddling
        the log
its wide paws
clutched. Immobile
    as myth's Dragon-
    guard beneath its
dangling wattle
    and its horny folds
of skin. That autumn
        Sunday
when my life
    had tunneled
back—forever—
    to some deep and
pristine torpor of my
        own: like

the grafting of my
    spirit onto hers,
there, in that cold
    autumnal prism
of sun glinting off
    my glasses, glowing
also from her stolid
    silver eyes—
black-circled craters
    of some distant
    point in time
our substance
    joined, then slowly
altered form. Those
    eyes that *may* have
seen me, also,
    as both our breaths
    rose foggy, on
that brilliant
cold Sunday, there,
    in Washington
National Zoo.

Dabney Stuart

Jesse Andrews

A Richmond, Virginia, native born in 1937, Dabney Stuart has taught English for more than thirty years at Washington and Lee University. He has been awarded fellowships from the Guggenheim Foundation, the National Endowment for the Arts, and the Rockefeller Foundation, and was the first writer to receive the Governor's Award of Virginia. Mr. Stuart's fourteen books of poetry include Settlers *(1999),* Long Gone *(1996), and* Light Years: New and Selected Poems *(1994), all from Louisiana State University Press. His third collection of short fiction,* No Visible Means of Support, *was published by the University of Missouri Press in 2001.*

Sleepwalker

The questionable old man wanders
the refuse dump, the railroad yards,
in his head, deserted, gets out of bed,
traverses the room, goes down the stairs,
his pajama shirttail flapping,
the thin cotton pressing his legs.
Look at that shin—razor sharp:
barefoot to the wind, no more regard.
I meet him coming
out of the front door at midnight.
He points his finger at the moon,
pulls the trigger. I ask him
where he's going. *Off* he says.
The upstairs bedroom sucks at him
through its open window, a vacuum cleaner;
his hair flows toward it. He lifts
his arms, grabs a low branch of the maple,
hauls himself up. Moonbird,
limbnestle. The tree vibrates

from the suction. At its top finally,
he hooks his toes into the ruff,
flaps his arms, flies with the tree
his wake, gone. The bedroom window
shudders, a mouth moaning.
I sit down in the great rootgap
his takeoff has left me, his will,
hoping to die in such arms.

The Man Who Loved Cezanne

> So I close this errant hand.
> —Cezanne

He liked the curve of Cezanne's thumb,
the end of it where the world moved.
He could ease it through the air
against one side of a brush, and the brush
would seem hardly to touch anything.
Sometimes it would poise and float
as if it didn't even touch his thumb.
He liked that particularly. It became
for him a way out of himself, and for Cezanne, too,
a way out, though the image
of the suspended brush might not have been
Cezanne's at all. It might be no one's.
He liked the way the canvas and paint box
settled compactly against Cezanne's back
as he walked the road near Auver—dusty,
one dry, focused shape, compact himself,
hugging with his inestimable hands
the upper end of a walking stick
on which he seemed to lean hardly at all.
Thirty-two years later, a little heavier
but still outdoors, on the road, dressed in a black
suit and fedora, he leans his canvas
against a rough stone wall. He liked to read

of the last years at Chemin des Lauves,
of Cezanne's dissatisfaction with his work,
never getting into the paint the vision
of his eye, so that Nature kept on being,
in spite of his most exquisite, deft strokes,
impermanent and impervious. Cezanne
didn't like that, or his neighbors' scorn,
or coffee without sugar. He was someone
you could trust. Near the end he began
to make only little fades of color
here and there, and then—an afterthought—
or a gesture of courtesy to us,
to his memory of Aix before art intervened—
he'd pencil a line or two of structure in,
trace the curve of a bridge,
or buttocks, or the flat bole of a pine.
Everything began to wash, and it rained
suddenly, the landscape and whole air
becoming watercolor you could almost breathe.

The Amber Window

He watches it hang in the air
like a canvas within
a Magritte canvas,
but it's no mirror
of anything, real or otherwise,
nor a repetition
of a thought, or an intimation.
Life of any other kind
doesn't surround it.
He knows the amber
derives from implausible pressure,
deep time,
but can't tell how
he sees it as the way he sees.
In the early morning

light passes into it, from it.
The father of the man watching
who has been undone once again
is sitting behind it,
settled in the long unleafing
of his own unhappiness.
His inspired patience
is the keeping of a promise.
It becomes his face.

Hidden Meanings

for Bob Denham

Both Hansel and Jack hated their mothers:
Jack sold the old cow
so she threw his seeds away;
Hansel let her feel his fingers a lot
and then stuffed her in the oven.
Their fathers were troublesome, too:
one was a wimp willing to sacrifice
his children; the other was so big
he had to be cut down, stalk first.
We know nothing about Rumpelstiltskin's
parents, but he played by himself in the woods
and when he couldn't get a baby by proxy
stuck his wooden leg through the floor.
The two boys finally got rich, like Cinderella,
but beyond that the ends are obscure.
Maybe they entered life, and found it to be
its own magic fable, as consequential
as any *Snow White Blood Red*,
and on the surface, true.

Eleanor Ross Taylor

*Born in North Carolina in 1920, Eleanor Ross Taylor
has lived in Charlottesville, Virginia, since 1967. She
was the recipient of the Shelly Memorial Prize from
the Poetry Society of America in 1997 and won the
Aiken-Taylor Award from the* Sewanee Review *in
2001. Her five volumes of poetry are* Wilderness of
Ladies *(1960),* Welcome Eumenides *(1972),* New
and Selected Poems *(1983),* Days Going/Days
Coming Back *(1992), and* Late Leisure *(1999),
which received the Library of Virginia Poetry Book
of the Year Award.*

August Doves

Haze
The garden stops to catch
its breath   a swallow-

    tail's reconnaissance   a
    sense of Canada   Alaska

too   the North Pole   but
the doves have brought a young
one to the flower bed
sliding trompe l'oeil among

the columbines come out
at iris   new one
flings wings across a stepping-stone

    panning damp edges'
    flicking-gold-tipped grubs
    a banner in sun-
    shine   a vernal sheen   won't

take a hint   the two   keep
noiselessly cross-sweeping

    not a word   their nest-
    frayed wings glint rusty
    rounds to high first-loosening leaves

Shaking the Plum Tree

Such light there was.
Ben up the plum tree,
   red plums snaked with light,
gold veins jagging in the plum skins
   like metal boiling,
plums bolting, knocking, to the ground,
   the sky, a huge shade-tree of light
tenting the stubblefield with centigrade,
   the pine woods' lashes, glass,
the girls' frocks, pale with glare,
   the voile geraniums, fading,
only the sheer hats shading
   the jelly cheeks dark red
and the simmering eyes,
   coming to a boil.

Deer

Six long-time friends Scotch-
   drinking dusk to night.
       Two fawns, it seems—
      hard to make out—
     male and female,
    shrub by shrub
over long grounds, halt in plain sight.

Can he see in?
    Those running leaps.
        At us?
        Wan boozers
        in soft chairs?
He paws and leaps and nears. She grazes on.

Our small fire's out,
    canes on the floor.
        We rise.
        This something
        targeting our dusk,
        our auld lang glass?
        This something knows
something it has to do—
shatter a wall and jump through.

The Sky-Watcher

Prowlers
    have scared the stars away.
She sets
    her outside light for six;
her neighbor
    burns his all night every night.
The city
    sends a van with a lift-basket
and a man
    to change street bulbs by schedule.

Some mornings,
    in the so-called dark, she gives up
searching
    Venus between chimneys and
massed leaves,
    turns out the lamps, and sits

147

with all
    the shades up in the living room.
Vast frames
    of light hang on the walls.
Umbrella
    and cane handles rise, gibbous,
in expanses
    unexplained. She watches the
fluorescent rays
    from kitchen louvers crosshatch
bookshelves,
    emitting black dimensions, stygian
and pure.
    A chair projects a symbol,
malformed,
    on the floor, and Berenice's Hair,
blowing
    somewhere, showers her human arm.

Late Leisure

Some things achieve finale;
vivace to larghetto;
three hundred pages, *End;*
threescore and ten, of course,
     that's it.

But this embroidery that I
inch aimlessly along
could be found years from now
wadded unfinished
     in a basket.

I, past my expiration date,
fold the cloth twice for center,
my needle threaded for the first

small stitch, myself
          capriciously ongoing.

I see it, as a sampler, challenging.
It has a long, protracted feel—
the dog each morning barking at the gate,
just where I left him
          yesterday.

I'll flesh out by the millimeter
a gawky shepherdess,
a time-lapse Federal house beyond,
odd birds and fish to signify
          earth floundering on,

the alphabet that's used
for English, French, Italian—
more tongues than I will speak
in this life, but fewer than birdcalls
          I recognize.

I'll work through color changes
almost photosynthetic;
I'll search out chairs by windows
in south-facing rooms;
          I'll never work by artificial light.

The sun won't cast a shadow of these men.
The curly beasts submit to cubist life
as in some static dream
the dead dream in their sleep,
          some plastic intervention.

If I get to the last rows
of this kit, I'll have to find
another one as slow and interim;
          but no need plan that yet.

Henry Taylor

Henry Taylor, born in Loudoun County, Virginia, in 1942, received degrees from the University of Virginia and Hollins College and is now a professor of literature and codirector of the M.F.A. program in creative writing at the American University in Washington, D.C. His six collections of poetry from Louisiana State University Press include The Flying Change, *for which he received the Pulitzer Prize in 1986,* Brief Candles (2000), Understanding Fiction (Poems 1986–1996), *and* The Horse Show at Midnight *(1966). He is also the author of* Compulsory Figures: Essays on Recent American Poets.

The Hayfork

I could get up from this kitchen table, I think,
and go see for myself whether, even now,
in the worn planks of the old barn floor,
there might be two holes I saw made there
forty years ago, in a single second along
the ponderous time-line of farming. Well,

I might get over there one of these days.
Meanwhile, what can I see from here? We entered
the barn's second story through a big sliding door
at the top of an earthen ramp. There was a haymow
on either side of a wagon-wide aisle-way.
A rail under the ridgepole ran gable to gable.

High in a dark far end, when I was a boy,
the old hayfork still hung there, barely visible
in cobwebs and thin strips of sunlight
that burst between weathering boards. Shaped
like a three-foot inverted U, a giant staple,
it rusted toward absolute darkness against which

stark blobs left by last season's mud-wasps
stood out like white spots on a heifer.
Who knew how long it had been there? Loose hay
was giving way to bales before I was born,
though here and there I've seen it made, the teams
of work-horses pulling the loader and wagon,

a man with a pitchfork working everyday magic
on top of the rack, the slow ride to the barn,
drawing the load up under the rail and the trip-stop.
A man dragged the fork down, hauling against
the tow-rope's weight the forty pounds of steel
with two barbed ends that grabbed the wads of hay.

Then the team, unhitched from the wagon, pulled
on the tow-rope, moving away from the barn,
lifting the hay toward the roof. A click
as the trolley-hook caught, then the hay
rode back along the rail into the mow
where men forked it away for the winter.

So to a day when I was twelve or thirteen,
when the baled hay we were making was plentiful,
stacked in the mow almost up to the roof,
and we were standing around in the aisle-way
after the wagon backed out, catching breath,
getting ready to go back to the field. One man

up in the mow took a notion and snatched
at the tag-end of rope still fastened to the hayfork,
so it whirred down the track to a place just above
the middle of the aisle-way, hit the trip, and dropped,
all faster, it seemed, than the noise of the track
could make us look up, and plunged its two points

into the floor just beside the left foot of Joe Trammel,
who stood there, leaning away from it, looking down
and then up, and around at all of us, a barnful

of men struck reverently silent in the presence
of whatever it was, the good luck that kept Joe
from injury, the bad luck that gave him his worst scare

in years, the innocent thoughtlessness that led
to that yank on the rope, the way things can go
for years without happening, biding their time
in a dust-whirling, cobwebby barn I can see
and smell and hear right now, staring down
at the grain in the wood of this kitchen table.

At South Fork Cemetery

It had no voice, or anything like that,
as it came across a field to where we stood
cleaning up an overgrown burial ground —
a quiet whirlwind we could see was there
by leaves it spiraled higher than the trees.

It slapped a leaf or two against our bodies,
then wandered on across the empty road.
As if the thoughtless world were generous,
we took that quirk of air as something given,
and turned to cutting brush and righting stones.

Tradition and the Individual Talent

An old-school foxhunter let it get around
that he hunted a deer-proof pack. Hard to believe:
foxhounds are born to run foxes, all right,
but you have to make them stay off rabbits,
housecats, chickens, etc. They learn to stop
when the hound-whip cracks. Deer scent, though,
is strong enough to put whips out of their minds.

So, somebody asked, how do you do it?
Take a bag of deer scent and a hound,
put them both in a fifty-five-gallon oil drum,
and roll it down a hill or a rocky road.
God almighty. You claim this really works?
Seems to. One thing I'll say's for damn sure:
they stay away from fifty-five-gallon drums.

Barbed Wire

One summer afternoon when nothing much
was happening, they were standing around
a tractor beside the barn while a horse
in the field poked his head between two strands
of the barbed-wire fence to get at the grass
along the lane, when it happened—something

they passed around the wood stove late at night
for years, but never could explain—someone
may have dropped a wrench into the toolbox
or made a sudden move, or merely thought
what might happen if the horse got scared, and
then he did get scared, jumped sideways and ran

down the fence line, leaving chunks of his throat
skin and hair on every barb for ten feet
before he pulled free and ran a short way
into the field, stopped and planted his hoofs
wide apart like a sawhorse, hung his head
down as if to watch his blood running out,

almost as if he were about to speak
to them, who almost thought he could regret
that he no longer had the strength to stand,
then shuddered to his knees, fell on his side,
and gave up breathing while the dripping wire
hummed like a bowstring in the splintered air.

Artichoke

> If poetry did not exist, would you
> have had the wit to invent it?
> —Howard Nemerov

He had studied in private years ago
the way to eat these things, and was prepared
when she set the clipped green globe before him.
He only wondered (as he always did
when he plucked from the base the first thick leaf,
dipped it into the sauce and caught her eye
as he deftly set the velvet curve against
the inside edges of his lower teeth
and drew the tender pulp toward his tongue
while she made some predictable remark
about the sensuality of this act
then sheared away the spines and ate the heart)
what mind, what hunger, first saw this as food.

The Flying Change

1

The canter has two stride patterns, one on the right lead and one on
the left, each a mirror image of the other. The leading foreleg is
the last to touch the ground before the moment of suspension
in the air. On cantered curves, the horse tends to lead with the
inside leg. Turning at liberty, he can change leads without effort
during the moment of suspension, but a rider's weight makes this
more difficult. The aim of teaching a horse to move beneath you
is to remind him how he moved when he was free.

2

A single leaf turns sideways in the wind
in time to save a remnant of the day;

I am lifted like a whipcrack to the moves
I studied on that barbered stretch of ground,
before I schooled myself to drift away

from skills I still possess, but must outlive.
Sometimes when I cup water in my hands
and watch it slip away and disappear,
I see that age will make my hands a sieve;
but for a moment the shifting world suspends

its flight and leans toward the sun once more,
as if to interrupt its mindless plunge
through works and days that will not come again.
I hold myself immobile in bright air,
sustained in time astride the flying change.

Riding Lesson

I learned two things
from an early riding teacher.
He held a nervous filly
in one hand and gestured
with the other, saying, "Listen.
Keep one leg on one side,
the other leg on the other side,
and your mind in the middle."

He turned and mounted.
She took two steps, then left
the ground, I thought for good.
But she came down hard, humped
her back, swallowed her neck,
and threw her rider as you'd
throw a rock. He rose, brushed
his pants and caught his breath,
and said, "See, that's the way
to do it. When you see
they're gonna throw you, get off."

Eric Trethewey

Eric Trethewey was born in Nova Scotia in 1943 and currently teaches creative writing at Hollins University. His books include The Long Road Home *(Goose Lane 1994) and* Evening Knowledge *(1991) and* Dreaming of Rivers *(1984), both from Cleveland State University Press. His poems have also appeared in many journals, including* Poetry, Southern Humanities Review, *the* Atlantic Monthly, *and the* New Republic.

Postbellum

Conceding the futility of anger,
this wet morning settles in all the way—

a small mound of ashes at field's edge,
carried here from the house and dumped;

or the spang of metal, rage's dull echo
resounding here in leafless solitude.

Cows drift single file across the hillside,
rocking heads heading nowhere in particular,

and on a flat rock at my feet, a beetle
flipped upside down, legs soliciting

the air, agitate the gourd of its body,
wavering, however slightly, in place.

Irony in the Teaching of *Oedipus Tyrannus*

Outrageous? Certainly. That any man,
knowingly or not, should butcher father

at a lonely crossroads, marry mother,
breed upon her children and brethren.

It's a tale difficult to understand,
except, perhaps, for those who can't read
books and never feel the baffling need
to know truth on a page. For them a damned

king is simply fact, and the gap between word
and flesh is the forgetting of acts long ago
in an old country. Still, the plot might echo
the daily grief by which they earn their bread.

Discovering *hubris*, those more literate
can point out precisely a *tyrant's* flaw,
indict him sure for what he couldn't know
and worse, the way he didn't know it.

Or, puzzling fate, they'll muse on why,
once announced, it can never be revoked.
(A matter of metaphysics they'll suspect.)
Stately in the pride of words, their high

sense of import in a phrase, some may take
longer than others to see the meaning
of ruthless disclosures concerning a king,
a noble man, if rash. For his parents' sake

and his own, he strove to avoid his fate
by relinquishing privilege: he left home,
riddled with a Sphinx. If he had known
what is only learned by living, of course too late,

he would not have had to reckon in arrears
for ignorance words may shield one from for years.

Lisa J. Parker

Lyrae Van Clief-Stefanon

Winner of the 2001 Cave Canem prize for her
first book, Black Swan *(University of Pittsburgh*
2002), Lyrae Van Clief-Stefanon was educated at
Washington and Lee University and Penn State
University. She has received an individual arts
grant from the Money for Women/Barbara
Deming Memorial Fund and currently offers
poetry workshops through the Fairfax County
Adult Community Education program in
Fairfax, Virginia.

199 Lee Street

Where the macrameed owl,
dirty-white, fuzzing from rain,
with darkly surprised wood-knob eyes,
must have hung on the porch
until its ropes rotted,
where toad-holes pocked
the front yard and I wrenched
the cool damp faucet, a metal flower,
drove the green hose deep
to flood them out,
I stripped bark from trees in fat bands
down to the meat,
green-rimmed like melon-rind
and ultra-white, new wounds
I licked to taste the bitter.
An old address sings girlhood
when mosquito bites warned evening
and I marked their flat mounds
with fingernail x's, crickets scratched out
their first sharp notes, lost
in the house where I learned the red rug
against my chest, my knees
my tongue, and the back room's

stark patterned tile—
blue red blue white red blue—
and the scrape of the unplaned back door
and the sound of the tight fit
and the final hard clink of its frosted glass slats
disturbed, then shaken into place.

Daphne

Fear glistened
In the sweat
On my skin
Until it dried
And cracked
And darkened
My *Father,*
Save me!
Hovered
In humid air
Hung there until
The brown bark
Of prayer
Encased me
This is
What passes
For safety
Now stillness
Settles on me
Like long vines
And silence
Entwines me
Rooted
Mute.

Reetika Vazirani

Reetika Vazirani, born in Punjab, India, in 1962, was for three years the Bannister Writer-in-Residence at Sweet Briar College. She received a "Discovery" award from the Nation, *and her book* White Elephants *(Beacon 1996) received the Barnard New Women Poets Prize. Her second book,* World Hotel, *was published by Copper Canyon Press in 2002. Ms. Vazirani received her M.F.A. from the University of Virginia. She was the visiting writer-in-residence at the College of William and Mary for 2002–2003.*

Type A Personality

It was my one year anniversary dating him.
He was doting on me in his heated Alfa Romeo
on the way to the developers' holiday party
for advertisers, the press, and restaurant owners
where what I heard was *right place at the right time,*
it was either that or a recording of that on location—

that's what all these people said, *location, location,
location.* I loved his car so I listened to him
talk about his business all the time,
he obsessed over it as Romeo
did Juliet, *that* went way over my head; he was the owner
of a restaurant and superb at the cocktail party

circuit, it was cool to show up at a party
with him, he could talk with anyone about his location,
a really hot spot or otherwise why be an owner,
hot or you're screwed (that was the theme). Did I choose him
or did he ensnare me mentioning a Romeo
Gigli dress I'd look good in? Great! What time

could we go get it? When he got time
off which was never (did we ever go to a party
together or did it just seem like one in his Alfa Romeo),
that and the fact (did we live in the same location?)
that I liked so many things about him
(not least of which was that he was a restaurant owner)

but the fact that he was a restaurant owner
was exactly why he was busy all the time,
you felt done in by the success of him
you adored him like Henry Kissinger life-of-the-party,
Steven Spielberg on location,
a twentieth century composite of Romeo,

sun roof down seats all leather, he's driving, this Romeo,
you crazy, and he's either the proud owner
of the world's richest company in a dynamite location
or the Sultan of Brunei for moments at a time
in your head, it's incredible to party
as you please (imagine! to take him

or leave him means the whole package: his Alfa Romeo
and his cocktail party loop) & you are the owner,
and this is about time & location location location

It's Me, I'm Not Home

It's late in the city, and I'm fast asleep.
You will call again? Is that a fact? Did I hear
(hi, please leave a message after the beep)

you like Chekhov? You do? I clap
for joy. A loves B. B loves C, C's not here
in the city, it's late, and I'm fast asleep

dreaming if your face nears like a familiar map
of homelessness: old world / new hemisphere
(it's me leave a message after the beep),

then the challenge of romance flies in the final lap
of the relay, I pass the baton you disappear
into the city, it's late, and I'm fast asleep

with married men again, they always drop
by, so faithful to me, not to their wives; *they* never
leave a message after the beep.

In order to stay in touch I rarely pick up
the receiver. Habits prove we persevere.
It's late in the city, and I'm fast asleep,
please leave a message after the beep.

Nancy Crampton

Ellen Bryant Voigt

Ellen Bryant Voigt was born in 1943 in Chatham, Virginia. Her books of poems include Kyrie *(1995),* Two Trees *(1992),* The Lotus Flowers *(1987), and* The Forces of Plenty *(1983), all from Norton, and* Claiming Kin *(Wesleyan University 1976). She attended Converse College and the University of Iowa and now teaches in the M.F.A. program at Warren Wilson College. Ms. Voigt edited (with Gregory Orr)* Poets Teaching Poets: Self and the World *(University of Michigan 1996), and her book of essays on poetry,* The Flexible Lyric, *was published by the University of Georgia Press in 1999. She has received grants from the National Endowment for the Arts and the Guggenheim Foundation and lives in Cabot, Vermont.*

Farm Wife

Dark as the spring river, the earth
opens each damp row as the farmer
swings the far side of the field.
The blackbirds flash their red
wing patches and wheel in his wake,
down to the black dirt; the windmill
grinds in its chain rig and tower.

In the kitchen, his wife is baking.
She stands in the door in her long white
gloves of flour. She cocks her head and
tries to remember, turns like the moon
toward the sea-black field. Her belly
is rising, her apron fills like a sail.
She is gliding now, the windmill churns
beneath her, she passes the farmer,
the fine map of the furrows.

The neighbors point to the bone-white
spot in the sky.

       Let her float
Like a fat gull that swoops and circles,
before her husband comes in for supper,
before her children grow up and leave her,
before the pulley cranks her down
the dark shaft, and the church blesses
her stone bed, and the earth seals
its black mouth like a scar.

Jug Brook

Beyond the stone wall,
the deer should be emerging from their yard.
Lank, exhausted, they scrape at the ground
where roots and bulbs will send forth
new definitions. The creek swells in its ditch;
the field puts on a green glove.
Deep in the words, the dead ripen,
and the lesser creatures turn to their commission.

Why grieve for the lost deer,
for the fish that clutter the brook,
the kingdoms of midge that cloud its surface,
the flocks of birds that come to feed.
The earth does not grieve.
It rushes toward the season of waste—

On the porch the weather shifts,
the cat dispatches
another expendable animal from the field.
Soon she will go inside to cull her litter,
addressing each with a diagnostic tongue.
Have I learned nothing? God,

into whose deep pocket our cries are swept,
it is you I look for
in the slate face of the water.

Soft Cloud Passing

1

Ice goes out of the pond as it came in—
from the edges toward the center:

large translucent pupil of an eye.

If the dream is a wish,
what does she wish for?

Soft cloud passing between us and the sun.

2

The plucked fields,
the bushes, spent and brittle,
the brown thatch on the forest floor
swoon beneath the gathered layers of gauze
before the earth is dragged once more into blossom.

And the woman at the window, watching the snow,
news of the child just now upon her—
she has the enviable rigor of the selfish,
light that seems so strong because withheld.
Already she cannot recall her former life.
She puts her face against the glass
as though listening.

Deer yarded up in the bog,
dogpack looking for deer.

The child is hot to her hand, less on his white
forehead beneath the damp foliage of hair
than in the crevices of thigh, belly, knee, dumpling-foot.
The telephone on the desk is a lump of coal.
She fans him with a magazine, she sponges
his limbs, her hands move up and down
as if ironing: this is how she prays,
without a sound, without closing her eyes.
When daylight was first sufficient to see the snow
falling, fine as sugar, it seemed an answer,
God chilling the world to save a child,
although she knows that isn't how it works.
Her husband naps in a chair;
doctor three blocks over, drugstore on the corner—
how often she walked past, pushing the stroller.
She lifts the baby closer to her heart.
The streets are clear, the sky clear, the sun
radiant and climbing:
the shelf of her breast will have to be the snow.
And so she holds him tighter, tighter,
believes she feels him cooling in her arms.

Nancy Crampton

Charles Wright

*Charles Wright was born in Pickwick Dam,
Tennessee, in 1935 and educated at Davidson
College and the University of Iowa. While serving
in the U.S. Army, he was stationed in Verona,
Italy. Since 1983 he has taught at the University of
Virginia, where he is Souder Family Professor of
English. He has received National Endowment for
the Arts and Guggenheim fellowships, as well as the
National Book Award (for* Country Music *in 1982),
the PEN Translation Prize (for* The Storm and
Other Things *in 1978), and the Pulitzer Prize and
the National Book Critics Circle Award (both for*
Black Zodiac). *Among his many books are* A Short
History of the Shadow *(2002) and* Negative Blue:
Selected Later Poems *(2000), both from Farrar,
Straus and Giroux.*

Dog Creek Mainline

Dog Creek: cat track and bird splay,
Spindrift and windfall; woodrot;
Odor of muscadine, the blue creep
Of kingsnake and copperhead;
Nightweed; frog spit and floating heart,
Backwash and snag pool: Dog Creek

Starts in the leaf reach and shoal run of the blood;
Starts in the falling light just back
Of the fingertips; starts
Forever in the black throat
You ask redemption of, in wants
You waken to, the odd door:

Its sky, old empty valise,
Stands open, departure in mind; its three streets,
Y-shaped and brown,

Go up the hills like a fever;
Its houses link and deploy
—This ointment, false flesh in another color.

                              *
Five cutouts, five silhouettes
Against the American twilight; the year
Is 1941; remembered names
—Rosendale, Perry and Smith—
Rise like dust in the deaf air;
The tops spin, the poison swells in the arm:

The trees in their jade death-suits,
The birds with their opal feet,
Shimmer and weave on the shoreline;
The moths, like forget-me-nots, blow
Up from the earth, their wet teeth
Breaking the dark, the raw grain;

The lake in its cradle hums
The old songs: out of its ooze, their heads
Like tomahawks, the turtles ascend
And settle back, leaving their chill breath
In blisters along the bank;
Locked in their wide drawer, the pike lie still as knives.
                              *
Hard freight. It's hard freight
From Ducktown to Copper Hill, from Six
To Piled High: Dog Creek is on this line,
Indigent spur; cross-tie by cross-tie it takes
You back, the red wind
Caught at your neck like a prize:

(The heart is a hieroglyph;
The fingers, like praying mantises, poise
Over what they have once loved;
The ear, cold cave, is an absence,
Tapping its own thin wires;
The eye turns in on itself.

The tongue is a white water.
In its slick ceremonies the light
Gathers, and is refracted, and moves
Outward, over the lips,
Over the dry skin of the world.
The tongue is a white water.).

Clear Night

Clear night, thumb-top of a moon, a back-lit sky.
Moon-fingers lay down their same routine
On the side deck and the threshold, the white keys and the
    black keys.
Bird hush and bird song. A cassia flower falls.

I want to be bruised by God.
I want to be strung up in a strong light and singled out.
I want to be stretched, like music wrung from a dropped seed.
I want to be entered and picked clean.

And the wind says "What?" to me.
And the castor beans, with their little earrings of death, say "What?"
    to me.
And the stars start out on their cold slide through the dark.
And the gears notch and the engines wheel.

Still Life on a Matchbox Lid

The heart is colder than the eye is.
The watchers, the holy ones,
                              know this, no shortcut to the sky.
A single dog hair can split the wind.

If you want great tranquility,

it's hard work and a long walk.
Don't brood on the past.
The word is without appendages,

no message, no name.

Deep Measure

Shank of the afternoon, wan weight-light,
Undercard of a short month,

February Sunday . . .
Wordlessness of the wrong world.
In the day's dark niche, the patron saint of What-Goes-Down
Shuffles her golden deck and deals,

one for you and one for me . . .

And that's it, a single number—we play what we get.
My hand says measure,

doves on the wire and first bulb blades
Edging up through the mulch mat,
Inside-out of the winter gum trees,
A cold harbor, cold stop and two-step, and here it comes,

Deep measure,

deep measure that runnels beneath the bone,
That sways our attitude and sets our lives to music;
Deep measure, down under and death-drawn:
Pilgrim, homeboy of false time,
Listen and set your foot down,

listen and step lightly.

A Bad Memory Makes You a Metaphysician,
A Good One Makes You a Saint

This is our world, high privet hedge on two sides,
                              half-circle of arborvitae,
Small strip of sloped lawn,
Last of the spring tulips and off-purple garlic heads
Snug in the cutting border,
Dwarf orchard down deep at the bottom of things,
                                        God's crucible,
Bat-swoop and grab, grackle yawp, back yard . . .

This is our landscape,
Bourgeois, heartbreakingly suburban;
                        these are the ashes we rise from.
As night goes down, we watch it darken and disappear.
We push our glasses back on our foreheads,
                        look hard, and it disappears.

In another life, the sun shines and the clouds are motionless.
There, too, the would-be-saints are slipping their hair shirts on.
But only the light souls can be saved;
Only the ones whose weight
                        will not snap the angel's wings.
Too many things are not left unsaid.
If you want what the syllables want, just do your job.

The Appalachian Book of the Dead IV

High-fiving in Charlottesville.
Sunset heaped up, as close to us as a barrel fire.
Let's all go down to the river,
            there's a man there that's walking on water,
On the slow, red Rivanna,
He can make the lame walk, he can make the dumb talk,
                        and open up the eyes of the blind.
That dry-shod, over-the-water walk.

Harbor him in your mind's eye, snub him snug to your hearts.

They'll have to sing louder than that.
                                  They'll have to dig deeper into the earbone
For this one to get across.
They'll have to whisper a lot about the radiant body.
Murmur of river run, murmur of women's voices.
Raised up, without rhyme,
                              the murmur of women's voices.
Good luck was all we could think to say.

Dogwood electrified and lit from within by April afternoon
   late-light,

This is the lesson for today—
                              narrative, narrative, narrative . . .
Tomorrow the sun comes back.
Tomorrow the tailings and slush piles will turn to gold
When everyone's down at the river.
The muscadines will bring forth,
The mountain laurel and jack-in-heaven,
                                 while everyone's down at the river.

The Appalachian Book of the Dead VI

Last page, The Appalachian Book of the Dead,
                                            full moon,
No one in anyone's arms, no lip to ear, cloud bank
And boyish soprano out of the east edge of things.
Ball-whomp and rig-grind stage right,
Expectancy, quivering needle, at north-northwest.

And here comes the angel with her drum and wings. Some wings.
Lost days, as Meng Chiao says, a little window of words
We peer through darkly. Darkly,
Moon stopped in cloud bank, light slick for the chute and long slide,

No lip, no ear.
        Distant murmur of women's voices.

I hear that the verb is facilitate. To facilitate.
Azure. To rise. To rise through the azure. Illegible joy.
No second heaven. No first.
I think I'll lie here like this awhile, my back flat on the floor.
I hear that days bleed.
        I hear that the right word will take your breath away.

Freezing Rain

Cold snare taps on the skylight,
           ice like a new conk on the trees,
Winter's slick-back and stiff gel,
Streetlamp reflections like vogueing boys
           doing the neighborhood.

Unlike the stars, herded together in their dark yard,
Programmed, unalterable,
           outriders sketched and firmed in.
Unlike their processed and guttering constellations.

There is an order beyond form,
           but not there. Not here, either.

Acknowledgments

Talvikki Ansel: "John Clare" and "Study Skins" by permission of Yale University Press.

Jennifer Atkinson: "The Dogwood Tree" and "Sky Shows around the Edges" by permission of the University of Alabama Press. "Three Years: A Composition in Gesso and Graphite" by permission of the author.

Molly Bendall: "A Shade Away" and "Bird Talk" by permission of the author.

Kelly Cherry: "On Watching a Young Man Play Tennis" by permission of the author. "Epithalamium" by permission of Louisiana State University Press.

Michael Chitwood: "Thinking of Rome in Fair Lea, West Virginia" and "Weave Room" by permission of the author.

Rosanne Coggeshall: "Jets" and "Prayer for the Whole State" by permission of Louisiana State University Press.

Stephen Cushman: "View from Lee's Camp" and "Second Opinion" by permission of Louisiana State University Press.

Richard Dillard: "Poe at the End" by permission of Louisiana State University Press. "The Mullins Farm" by permission of the author.

Gregory Donovan: "The Grandfather in the Rafters" and "Runes" by permission of the author.

Rita Dove: "Parsley," "The Event," and "Taking in Wash" by permission of the author. "Canary" by permission of W. W. Norton.

Claudia Emerson: "Auction," "Plagues," "The Taxidermist," and "The Admirer" by permission of Louisiana State University Press.

Forrest Gander: "Field Guide to Southern Virginia" by permission of New Directions Publishing Corporation.

George Garrett: "Figure of Speech," "The Long and the Short of It," and "Main Currents of American Political Thought" by permission of Louisiana State University Press.

Margaret Gibson: "Earth Elegy" and "Keeping Still" by permission of

Louisiana State University Press. "Presque Isle" by permission of the author.

Nikki Giovanni: "Knoxville, Tennessee" and "Nikki-Rosa" by permission of the author.

John Haines: "The Stone Harp," "The Weaver," and "Brand" by permission of Graywolf Press.

Cathryn Hankla: "Encounter" by permission of the author. "On Athena's Shoulder" by permission of Louisiana State University Press.

Henry Hart: "Pocahontas in Jamestown" by permission of University of Illinois Press. "Notes from Mount Vernon" by permission of the author.

David Huddle: "Threshing Wheat," "Study," and "Model Father" by permission of Louisiana State University Press.

T. R. Hummer: "Heresies, Overheard," "Zeitgeist Lightning," and "Friendly Fire" by permission of the author.

Julia Johnson: "October in Virginia" and "The Drive" by permission of Louisiana State University Press.

Sam Kashner: "Vehemence & Opinions" and "Unidentifiable in Rain" by permission of the author.

Sally Keith: "The Hunters" by permission of the author.

Sarah Kennedy: "Flow Blue" and "Ewe" by permission of Elixir Press. "Sin" by permission of the author.

Peter Klappert: "Bright Moments Lakeside" and "Chokecherries" by permission of the author.

Jeanne Larsen: "Turning the Edge" and "After the Rains" by permission of the author.

Edward C. Lynskey: "In Search of Our Father's Guitar and Gin" and "Persephone in West Virginia" by permission of the author.

Heather Ross Miller: "Cloudless Sulfur, Swallowtail, Great Spangled Fritillary," "Good Colds," and "Sleepwalker" by permission of the author.

Elizabeth Seydel Morgan: "Swing, Boat, Table" and "At Epidaurus" by permission of the author.

Debra Nystrom: "The Cliff Swallows" and "Emily's Ghost" by permission of the author.

Gregory Orr: "Like Any Other Man," "Leaving the Asylum," "We Must Make a Kingdom of It," and "Celestial Desolations" by permission of the author.

Eric Pankey: "Nostalgia" by permission of Alfred A. Knopf. "Crab Apple" and "A Walk with My Father" by permission of the author.

Jim Peterson: "Fish to Fry" and "Not Talking at Dawn" by permission of the author.

Hermine Pinson: "Left-Handed Poem" by permission of the author.

Lucinda Roy: "The Curtsy" and "The Virginia Reel" by permission of Eighth Mountain Press.

Steve Scafidi: "On Looking into Golding's Ovid," "To Whoever Set My Truck on Fire," and "Ode to Rosa Parks" by permission of Louisiana State University Press.

Nancy Schoenberger: "Nathaniel Hawthorne in Hell" and "Long like a River" by permission of the author.

Tim Seibles: "Latin" by permission of the author.

Dana Littlepage Smith: "Asherah" and "The Widow and Her Mite" by permission of Louisiana State University Press.

Dave Smith: "Night Pleasures," "Canary Weather in Virginia," "Crab House," "On a Field Trip at Fredericksburg," "Near the Docks," and "Of Oystermen, Workboats" by permission of Louisiana State University Press.

R. T. Smith: "Alphabet" by permission of Louisiana State University Press. "Zion, Vernacular Exposure, Mockingbird Song" and "Scavenging the Wall" by permission of the author.

Ron Smith: "Leaving Forever" and "Photograph of Jesse Owens at the Gun" by permission of the author.

Katherine Soniat: "Apricots and Oranges" and "Pressure" by permission of the author.

Lisa Russ Spaar: "Rapunzel at 14," and "April" by permission of Red Hen Press.

Dan Stryk: "Spirit of Komodo" by permission of the author.

Dabney Stuart: "Sleepwalker," "The Amber Window," and "Hidden Meanings" by permission of Louisiana State University Press. "The Man Who Loved Cezanne" by permission of the author.

Eleanor Ross Taylor: "August Doves," "Shaking the Plum Tree," "Deer," "The Sky-Watcher," and "Late Leisure" by permission of Louisiana State University Press.

Henry Taylor: "The Hayfork" by permission of the author. "At South Fork Cemetery," *"Tradition and the Individual Talent,"* "Barbed Wire," "Artichoke," "The Flying Change," and "Riding Lesson" by permission of Louisiana State University Press.

Eric Trethewey: "Postbellum" and "Irony in the Teaching of *Oedipus Tyrannus*" by permission of the author.

Lyrae Van Clief-Stefanon: "199 Lee Street" and "Daphne" by permission of the author.

Reetika Vazirani: "Type A Personality" and "It's Me, I'm Not Home" by permission of the author.

Ellen Bryant Voigt: "Farm Wife" by permission of Wesleyan University